YAS

W9-AFQ-509

Kidnapping

by Jan Burns

LUCENT BOOKS
A part of Gale, Cengage Learning

GALE
CENGAGE Learning™

Detroit • New York • San Francisco • New Haven, Conn • Waterville, Maine • London

© 2008 Gale, a part of Cengage Learning

For more information, contact
Lucent Books
27500 Drake Rd.
Farmington Hills, MI 48331-3535
Or you can visit our Internet site at gale.cengage.com

LIBRARY OF CONGRESS CATALOGING-IN-PUBLICATION DATA

Burns, Jan.
  Kidnapping / by Jan Burns.
      p. cm. — (Crime scene investigations)
  Includes bibliographical references and index.
  ISBN 978-1-59018-989-4 (hardcover)
  1. Kidnapping—Juvenile literature. I. Title.
  HV6595.B87 2008
  363.25'954—dc22

                                                    2007040931

ISBN-10: 1-59018-989-2

Printed in the United States of America
 2 3 4 5 6 7 12 11 10 09 08

Contents

Foreword

The popularity of crime scene and investigative crime shows on television has come as a surprise to many who work in the field. The main surprise is the concept that crime scene analysts are the true crime solvers, when in truth, it takes dozens of people, doing many different jobs, to solve a crime. Often, the crime scene analyst's contribution is a small one. One Minnesota forensic scientist says that the public "has gotten the wrong idea. Because I work in a lab similar to the ones on CSI, people seem to think I'm solving crimes left and right—just me and my microscope. They don't believe me when I tell them that it's just the investigators that are solving crimes, not me."

Crime scene analysts do have an important role to play, however. Science has rapidly added a whole new dimension to gathering and assessing evidence. Modern crime labs can match a hair of a murder suspect to one found on a murder victim, for example, or recover a latent fingerprint from a threatening letter, or use a powerful microscope to match tool marks made during the wiring of an explosive device to a tool in a suspect's possession.

Probably the most exciting of the forensic scientist's tools is DNA analysis. DNA can be found in just one drop of blood, a dribble of saliva on a toothbrush, or even the residue from a fingerprint. Some DNA analysis techniques enable scientists to tell with certainty, for example, whether a drop of blood on a suspect's shirt is that of a murder victim.

While these exciting techniques are now an essential part of many investigations, they cannot solve crimes alone. "DNA doesn't come with a name and address on it," says the Minnesota forensic scientist. "It's great if you have someone in custody to match the sample to, but otherwise, it doesn't help.

That's the investigator's job. We can have all the great DNA evidence in the world, and without a suspect, it will just sit on a shelf. We've all seen cases with very little forensic evidence get solved by the resourcefulness of a detective."

While forensic specialists get the most media attention today, the work of detectives still forms the core of most criminal investigations. Their job, in many ways, has changed little over the years. Most cases are still solved through the persistence and determination of a criminal detective whose work may be anything but glamorous. Many cases require routine, even mind-numbing tasks. After the July 2005 bombings in London, for example, police officers sat in front of video players watching thousands of hours of closed-circuit television tape from security cameras throughout the city, and as a result were able to get the first images of the bombers.

The Lucent Books Crime Scene Investigations series explores the variety of ways crimes are solved. Titles cover particular crimes such as murder, specific cases such as the killing of three civil rights workers in Mississippi, or the role specialists such as medical examiners play in solving crimes. Each title in the series demonstrates the ways a crime may be solved, from the various applications of forensic science and technology to the reasoning of investigators. Sidebars examine both the limits and possibilities of the new technologies and present crime statistics, career information, and step-by-step explanations of scientific and legal processes.

The Crime Scene Investigations series strives to be both informative and realistic about how members of law enforcement—criminal investigators, forensic scientists, and others—solve crimes, for it is essential that student researchers understand that crime solving is rarely quick or easy. Many factors—from a detective's dogged pursuit of one tenuous lead to a suspect's careless mistakes to sheer luck to complex calculations computed in the lab—are all part of crime solving today.

A Single Clue

Thirteen-year-old William "Ben" Ownby disappeared on January 8, 2007, after he was dropped off by a school bus in Beaufort, Missouri. Mitchell Hults, one of Ben's classmates, rode the bus with him that afternoon. He remembered seeing a white compact Nissan pickup truck with a camper shell speeding away from the area. After investigators found a tire track at the scene that proved to be from a small Nissan truck, they concentrated on finding the vehicle.

On January 12, members of the Kirkwood, Missouri, police force spotted a white truck that matched the description of the suspect vehicle. After tracking it, they got a warrant and searched the apartment of Michael Devlin. Not only did they find Ben inside, they also found 15-year-old Shawn Hornbeck, who had been missing for four and a half years. The two boys were reunited with their families because the police followed up on a single clue.

While this kidnapping case was satisfactorily resolved, many others are not, with questions left unanswered years later.

The Crime of the Century

Charles Lindbergh became world famous in the 1930s after he became the first man to fly across the Atlantic Ocean solo in his single-engine plane, *Spirit of St. Louis*. When Lindbergh's son was kidnapped, the media called it the "crime of the century."

After his legendary flight, Lindbergh was widely regarded as a national hero. The press hounded him relentlessly. Desiring some privacy, he and his wife, Anne, built a home in

A single clue, such as tire tracks, left at the scene of a kidnapping can help police track down the perpetrator.

a remote New Jersey area called Hopewell. They stayed there on weekends. During the week, they lived at Anne's family's home in Englewood. But on the last weekend of February 1932, they remained in Hopewell a few extra days because their twenty-month-old son was sick.

Charles Lindbergh II, or Charlie, as his parents called him, was last seen sleeping in his bed in Hopewell, around 8 P.M. on March 1. When nanny Betty Gow checked on the child at 10 P.M., however, she discovered that he was missing. Lindbergh alerted the local police as well as the state police. Meanwhile, he searched the grounds armed with a loaded rifle.

State police officers soon arrived. Known to be strong on enforcement but weak on investigative skills, they started a frenzied, disorganized search. Before long they found a chisel, a homemade ladder, and some footprints. They neglected to measure or make plaster casts of the prints to preserve them as evidence. Initial reports claimed that two sets of footprints were found, but later reports said there was only one set. It

The high-profile kidnapping of Charles Lindbergh Jr. made national news and was on the cover of Time *magazine.*

is possible that one set was destroyed with all the police officers tramping about the grounds.

Corporal Frank Kelly went with Lindbergh and state police chief Norman Schwarzkopf to search the nursery. Lindbergh had seen an envelope on the windowsill but had been careful not to touch it. As Lindbergh had suspected, the envelope contained a ransom note. The kidnappers demanded $50,000 and warned Lindbergh not to contact the police. Kelly dusted this as well as other sections of the room for fingerprints but could not find any usable ones.

Lindbergh took control of the investigation. Schwarzkopf gave in to him, probably because of Lindbergh's hero status. Lindbergh turned down most of the advice law enforcement officials gave him. He protested repeatedly when detectives questioned his staff members about their whereabouts on the night of the kidnapping. He refused to have wiretaps put on his telephones so that calls from the kidnappers could be traced. He also ruled out any police surveillance when the ransom money was delivered, fearing this might prompt the kidnappers to kill his son.

When Lindbergh-admirer John Condon volunteered to act as a liaison between Lindbergh and the kidnappers, both sides agreed. Eventually Condon gave the ransom money to a man known as "Cemetery John." John indicated the child was on a boat nearby.

Investigators soon learned that Cemetery John was lying about Charlie Lindbergh's whereabouts. The baby's body was found badly decomposed on May 12, just 4 miles (6.5km) from his Hopewell home. The cause of death was a massive fracture of the skull. The coroner believed he had probably been killed the night he was kidnapped.

Luckily, the serial numbers of the ransom money had been recorded on a list that was widely distributed. The case broke open after an alert gas station attendant checked the serial number of a bill that a customer used to pay for gas. The attendant discovered the bill was ransom money. Illegal German immigrant Bruno Hauptmann was arrested on September 19, 1934. Soon afterward, police discovered more than $14,000 of the ransom money hidden in his garage. His claims that the money belonged to a former business partner who had returned to Germany were widely ignored. Then Arthur Koehler of the United States Forest Products Lab in Madison, Wisconsin, matched some wood from the rafters in Hauptmann's attic with that from the ladder found near the Lindbergh home on the night of the kidnapping. Hauptmann was convicted of kidnapping and murder and executed on January 13, 1936.

Former Federal Bureau of Investigation (FBI) special agent John Douglas believes it was a mistake to allow Lindbergh to dictate limitations to the police. He thinks if the police had been allowed to cover the money drop, they probably could have picked up Cemetery John. It wouldn't have saved Charlie

Lindbergh Law

On June 22, 1932, the U.S. Congress passed a law commonly known as the Lindbergh Law. It states that one week after an abduction, if the case remains unsolved, the kidnapper is presumed to have crossed state lines, and the Federal Bureau of Investigation (FBI) can then be given primary jurisdiction. The law also calls for a federal maximum penalty of life imprisonment.

A writing expert compared ransom notes sent to the Lindberghs with a handwriting sample from suspect Bruno Hauptmann. Hauptmann was later convicted of kidnapping and executed.

Lindbergh, but the case would have been solved. Douglas also says it was obvious that the criminals had insider information about the Lindbergh family. They knew that the Lindberghs planned to remain at Hopewell longer than usual because Charlie was sick. Douglas believes maid Violet Sharpe might have directly or indirectly passed this information on to the kidnappers.

Millions of pages of evidence, reports, and testimony about the case have been gathered, but doubts still remain as to how the kidnapping was carried out, and who really did it. Law enforcement officials point to this and emphasize that to have any hope of getting a kidnapped victim back alive, a crime scene investigation has to be controlled and organized from the very start.

CHAPTER 1

Is It Kidnapping?

There are a number of reasons it may be unclear whether a missing child has been kidnapped or not. Sometimes there are simple mix-ups as to where a child is supposed to be at a certain time, and the situation is easily resolved after a few phone calls. Some children run away. But in other situations, children are forcibly taken somewhere against their will. This is kidnapping, and it is a criminal offense. A critical first step is accurate assessment of the crime scene to determine whether a kidnapping has occurred.

Ruling Out Runaways

In a typical year, more than 800,000 U.S. children are reported missing, according to the United States Department of Justice. Most of them turn out to be runaways or victims of family abductions. Because of this, when a child is reported missing, law enforcement officials often first suspect he or she might have run away. They investigate this possibility before they consider other alternatives.

Police officer Darren Barnett says that parents should contact police as soon as they realize their child is missing. They can go directly to a police station or ask that an officer come to their home so they can report it. "Police would first ask them about their child's behavior. They would also want to know if they had a habit of leaving. Parents would also be asked if it's abnormal that their child hasn't called. Does their child usually check in if they've been out with their friends for awhile? Also, very importantly, police would ask if the parents have already checked with their child's friends, to see if they have heard from the missing person."[1]

Realistically, parents are not always aware of the problems or situations their child might be facing, especially when teenagers are involved. In those cases, friends are far more likely to know what was going on in the missing person's life, so the police want names and contact information for the missing child's friends so they can question them too.

The police try to find out whether anything happened recently that might have led to the individual's disappearance. Police ask about things such as arguments at home or whether the missing child was recently punished for something or whether he or she is having trouble at school. Police officers want to find out what the missing person's emotional state was like before the disappearance. From past experience, they know this can be a good indicator of what might have happened.

Missing person photos of children are frequently seen on posts in neighborhoods nationwide. According to the U.S. Department of Justice, over 800,000 American children are reported missing every year.

FBI Child Abduction Rapid Deployment Teams

FBI Child Abduction Rapid Deployment (CARD) teams are made up of FBI agents and analysts who have in-depth experience and a proven track record in crimes against children investigations, especially cases where a child has been abducted by someone other than a family member.

Relying on their expertise and experience, team members make sure that investigations move quickly, efficiently, and thoroughly. They provide the FBI field division that is running the investigation with on-site investigative, technical, and resource assistance during the initial critical period after a child has been kidnapped.

The teams are deployed soon after an abduction has been reported to a local FBI field office, to FBI headquarters, or to the National Center for Missing and Exploited Children or in any other cases when the FBI determines such an investigation is warranted.

There are eight regional teams nationwide: two each in the Northeast, the Southeast, Central United States, and the West. The FBI can send a team anywhere in the U.S. within hours.

www.fbi.gov/page2/june06/card_teams061606.htm

Especially when teens are involved, they also check to see whether the missing person visited any Internet chat rooms. The National Center for Missing and Exploited Children (NCMEC) suggests that "computers and other online devices should be checked as a source of leads or other information concerning people [a] child may have been communicating with. It may shed light on any planned meetings between [the] child and someone he or she 'met' online."[2] Checking the contents of e-mails can be especially enlightening.

Especially when teens are involved, the police will often check to see what Internet sites the missing person has visited, which could lead to a kidnapper's location.

Search for Evidence

Police say signs that a child might have planned to run away include if any clothing, money, or favorite possessions, such as a cell phone, are missing. They also ask parents whether their child kept a diary or journal. If so, writings inside might reveal whether the child was planning to leave. Alternately, if the diary is missing, it might be an indication that the child took it. If none of these things are missing, it would look like the child did not plan to run away. All these things may seem trivial, but when added together, they can provide parents and police with helpful information.

The circumstances of how a person disappeared can also point to what happened. If there are witnesses who saw the person being abducted against his or her will, they would naturally lead police to label it a kidnapping. If there are no witnesses, police officers might question whether a kidnapping actually occurred. They determine this on a case-by-case basis

National Crime Information Center

The National Crime Information Center (NCIC) is a nationwide information system dedicated to serving and supporting criminal justice agencies—local, state, and federal—in their mission to uphold the law and protect the public. It extends these services down to the patrol car and mobile officer.

Its capabilities include the following:
- Enhanced name search—Uses the N.Y. State Identification and Intelligence System (NYSIIS). Returns phonetically similar names (for example, Marko, Marco or Knowles, Nowles).
- Fingerprint searches—Stores and searches the right index fingerprint. Search inquiries compare the print to all fingerprint data on file (wanted persons and missing persons).
- Probation/parole—Convicted persons or supervised release file contains records of subjects under supervised release.
- Mug shots—One mug shot per record may be entered. One fingerprint, one signature, and up to ten other identifying images (scars, marks, tattoos) may also be entered.
- Convicted sex offender registry—Contains records of individuals who are convicted sexual offenders or violent sexual predators.
- SENTRY file—An index of individuals incarcerated in the federal prison system. Response provides descriptive information and location of prison.

www.fbi.gov/hq/cjisd/ncic.htm.

after finding out the circumstances surrounding the alleged kidnapping.

If it seems probable that a kidnapping has occurred, local authorities may ask the FBI for assistance. The FBI has Child Abduction Rapid Deployment (CARD) teams made up of agents and analysts with in-depth experience and proven track records in investigations of crimes against children. They also have a wide variety of resources that local law enforcement authorities probably do not have.

National Crime Information Center

It is vitally important that the missing person's name, description, date of birth, height, and weight be entered into the National Crime Information Center's (NCIC) nationwide computerized database of missing persons as soon as possible. At the same time, the information should also be entered into the state missing children's clearinghouse database. Police may also ask for a recent photo and get fingerprints and a DNA sample of the individual. This information will then be available to law enforcement agencies across the country. There is no longer any mandatory waiting period that has to elapse before this is done. If for any reason local authorities are hesitant to enter the

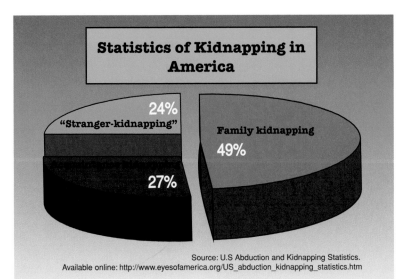

Statistics of Kidnapping in America

24% "Stranger-kidnapping"

Family kidnapping 49%

27%

Source: U.S Abduction and Kidnapping Statistics.
Available online: http://www.eyesofamerica.org/US_abduction_kidnapping_statistics.htm

information, the NCMEC advises parents to call the FBI themselves and ask that it be done.

Questioning the Parents

Law enforcement authorities question the parents about any possible role they might have played in their child's disappearance. This may seem bewildering to the parents, especially because they probably were the ones who reported it. From a police standpoint, however, the parents have to be ruled out as suspects before the police can move forward on other possible leads. If the parents seem reluctant to answer any of the questions they are asked, it may be a signal they have something to hide or have not told the whole story. They may also be asked to take a polygraph, or lie detector, test. Police sometimes consider reluctance to take the test as a sign of possible guilt.

The initial police investigation is extremely important because it determines whether an individual has actually been kidnapped. If the wrong decision is made, it can result in an individual's death. Parents and family members of some kidnapped victims have complained that failure by police to immediately declare that a kidnapping took place resulted in their child's death. Police, on the other hand, say they are not always able to do this because of reasonable doubt, and/or lack of physical evidence. They also say the large number of missing children cases makes it difficult to quickly assess some situations. This is particularly true in cities and towns where police departments are understaffed.

Parents are usually the first suspects when a missing child is reported. They often take a polygraph, or lie detector, test to rule themselves out as suspects and help move the investigation forward.

Importance of Accurate Assessment

One case in which a different initial police assessment might have led to a dramatically different ending involved fourteen-year-old Stephanie Bryan. On April 28, 1955, she walked home from school in Berkeley, California, with classmate Mary Ann Seward.

Hundreds of volunteers searched tirelessly for 14-year-old Stephanie Bryan after her disappearance in 1955.

Stephanie was last seen around 4:00 P.M. when she told her friend good-bye and took her usual shortcut home through the parking lot of the Claremont Hotel. However, she never made it home. When Stephanie had not arrived by 4:15 P.M., her mother called three of her daughter's friends and also went to the school. Stephanie was rarely late, so the mother was surprised and worried about where her daughter could be. Mrs. Bryan called her husband. He came home from work around 6:30 P.M., called police, and then started searching the neighborhood and the hotel grounds.

Earlier, at around 4:45 P.M., police in neighboring Contra Costa County received reports from people who saw a young girl struggling with a man in a car on Tunnel Road. This was only a few minutes away by car from the Claremont Hotel. By the time the police got there, though, the car was gone. Seven more reports from people who had witnessed this incident came in over the next twenty-four hours. One woman even reported that she had heard the girl give "a loud, horrible scream."[3] At first police did not associate these reports with the Bryans' missing person report.

Local police initially thought Stephanie was a runaway, although her father declared that "It is impossible to believe that she may be a runaway. … She is not that type of girl."[4] In fact, Stephanie got along quite well with her parents, was an outstanding student, and also was said to be reserved and shy around strangers.

However, few violent abductions took place in the 1950s. At the time, most of the teens who were reported missing usually turned out to be runaways. Because of this, local police were reluctant to start an immediate search that might prove to be unnecessary. There were also no eyewitnesses, the Bryans had not received a ransom demand for their daughter, and there was no evidence of interstate transportation, or explicit threat of bodily harm. These were the criteria that the police used at the time to judge whether a kidnapping had occurred.

A week after Stephanie's disappearance hundreds of volunteers, including members of the National Guard, spent thousands of hours searching the area around the Claremont Hotel and beyond, into the East Bay hills, searching for the girl. House-to-house searches were conducted around Contra Costa County, and local police mailed out 500 notices about Stephanie's kidnapping to law enforcement agencies throughout an eleven-state area. Finally, two weeks after Stephanie's disappearance, the FBI was called in to the case. By then, valuable time had been lost, and FBI experts who might have had the experience and resources to find her alive were called in too late to do any real good.

Identification Found

Various leads came in from all over the Berkeley area and beyond by people who claimed they had recently seen Bryan. They all proved to be dead ends until July 15. By that time, Stephanie's name and picture had been widely publicized. Georgia Abbott notified police that she had found the girl's purse and ID in the basement of her home. She and her twenty-seven year old husband, Burton "Bud" Abbott, and her husband's mother, Elsie Abbott, lived in Alameda, which was about a fifteen-minute drive from Berkeley. When police went to the home and interviewed the Abbotts, they discovered that Elsie Abbott had known for some time that Stephanie Bryan's purse was there.

"His mother found the wallet soon after the girl went missing," said Harry Farrell, a newspaper reporter who was covering the case. "I think what happened was, she didn't realize exactly the extent of what police were looking for and started talking about this to everybody, not realizing she was driving nails in her son's coffin."[5]

Detectives, led by Berkeley Police Department inspector Charles O'Meara, questioned Bud Abbott closely, but he denied any guilt. A search of his unfinished basement, though,

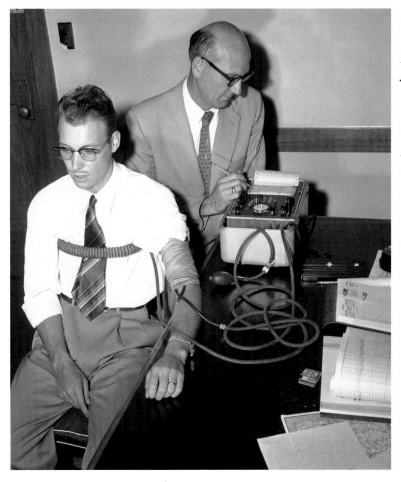

After several of Stephanie Bryan's possessions were found in his basement, Bud Abbott was questioned about her disappearance and given a lie detector test. After her body was found, Abbott was convicted of kidnapping and murder.

revealed library books, school notes, glasses, and a torn bra that had all belonged to Stephanie. However, police still couldn't find the girl's body. At the time, finding the body was considered critical to declare a person dead.

Abbott told police he had driven to California's remote Trinity Alps region, which was about 250 miles (400km) north of Berkeley, on the morning of the day that Stephanie had disappeared. Ed Montgomery, who was a reporter for the *San Francisco Examiner*, was sent to the area to see whether he could find anything associating Abbott to the kidnapping. He learned that the Abbotts had an old fishing cabin there, and he thought it might hold clues. As soon as he got to the cabin, he smelled something foul, but he could not detect exactly where the smell was coming from. He returned to the cabin the next day with a tracker and dogs that had been able to previously discover a missing body. The dogs took off right past Abbott's cabin, across a road, and up a slope to a spot where someone

Becoming an FBI Police Officer

Job Description:
The FBI maintains a force of uniformed police officers whose primary mission is to maintain law and order and to protect life, property, and the civil rights of bureau employees and visitors. They conduct patrols on foot and in vehicles to check for unsecured windows and doors, detect and prevent illegal entry, identify suspicious persons and vehicles, and respond to other conditions. When crimes are detected, officers secure crime scenes, collect and preserve evidence, interview victims and witnesses, and process prisoners.

Education:
Applicants must be high school graduates.

Qualifications:
Applicants must be at least 21 years of age, and possess a valid driver's license. Candidates must pass a physical examination, including eyesight and hearing tests. Applicants must complete an online application and submit additional information as requested.

Salary:
Starting salary is approximately $27,000. Applicants with additional education qualify for a higher starting salary.

had obviously been digging. When Montgomery scraped away some soil from the area with a shovel, he saw a brown-and-white shoe. He had found Stephanie's body buried in a shallow grave. He contacted Trinity County sheriff's deputies, who exhumed the corpse. Abbott was soon arrested on suspicion of kidnapping and murder.

Evidence Presented at Abbott's Trial

The 48-day trial, where more than a hundred people testified, made front-page headlines around the nation. Abbott's lawyers argued that the evidence against him was all circumstantial. To prove its case, the FBI checked more than 150,000 credit card purchases to determine when and where Abbott purchased gasoline during the time Stephanie had first gone missing and, with other law enforcement officers, interviewed more than three thousand people.

University of California criminalist Dr. Paul Kirk testified at Abbott's trial that an analysis of dirt clots from Abbott's boots matched the dirt from around the cabin, proving that Abbott had been there recently, which he had denied. Kirk also proved that strands of hair found in Abbott's car belonged to Stephanie. He testified that the chances that the hair belonged to someone other than the girl were one in 135,000. Alameda County forensic pathologist Dr. George Loquvam stated that Stephanie's death was due to a massive depression to the back of her skull. Abbott was convicted and later executed for Stephanie Bryan's kidnapping and murder. He protested that he was innocent up until his death.

Crime writer Marilyn Bardsley has researched this case, as well as others in which police were slow to believe that a missing person was ever in any real danger. She believes "Some victims could have been saved if the police had simply spent more time separating out suspicious disappearances of young people from probable runaways."[6]

Legislation

By the 1980s, there was a growing feeling among legislators and advocates for parents of kidnapped children that current laws were inadequate to deal with the increasing number of kidnapping cases. They worked to reform the legal system to stiffen the penalties for kidnapping and to be able to declare a person was missing earlier than before so law enforcers could immediately start a search.

Two pieces of legislation clearly define the law with respect to the disappearance of a child. The 1982 Missing Children's Act defines a missing child as "any individual younger than eighteen years of age whose whereabouts is unknown to their legal custodian." Circumstances must indicate that the disappearance happened without the custodian's consent, or the circumstances must strongly indicate that the child is likely to have been abused or sexually exploited.

The National Child Assistance Act of 1990 states that law enforcement agencies do not have to observe a waiting period before accepting a missing child case and that each missing child who is reported to law enforcement must be entered immediately into the state law enforcement system and National Crime Information Center.

Without a Trace

A small percentage of kidnapping victims completely disappear, and no trace of them is ever found. This was the case with ten-year-old Kevin Collins. After his Friday evening basketball practice on February 10, 1984, at St. Agnes School in San Francisco, California, he went to catch a bus home. It is believed he did not want to wait for a ride home with his coach, where he would have to ride with older kids who sometimes teased and punched him. People later said Kevin was really looking forward to a big basketball game the next day. He was last seen waiting at a bus stop around 7:00 P.M., talking to a tall blond man who had a large black dog with him.

When Kevin had not arrived home by 7:30 that evening, his father, David Collins, and his coach, Paul Fontana, searched the neighborhood. When they failed to find him, his father called the police. Police initially suspected that Kevin might have run away. Statistically, that was what most missing person cases involving children turned out to be. Kevin really did not fit the profile of a runaway, though. He was one of nine children in a close-knit Catholic family. His parents seemed grief-stricken about the disappearance and vowed to find him.

Kevin's parents later said they realized if they ever wanted to see their son again, they would have to work hard to get him back. They had to come up with their own ideas about how to alert the community to the kidnapping and to find volunteers to help them search for Kevin. David and Ann Collins worked tirelessly to get their son's picture and news of his kidnapping out and to organize hundreds of volunteers who conducted house-to-house searches.

To raise awareness about Kevin Collins' disappearance, thousands of posters were distributed throughout the neighborhood and plastered on poles, windows, and billboards.

Working with them was Kevin's uncle, Michael Deasy, a public affairs representative for the California Department of Transportation, who developed a public relations campaign. Within five days of Kevin's disappearance, two thousand posters had been printed and distributed through the two-hundred-block area around St. Agnes. Eventually, the number of posters printed would grow to hundreds of thousands. Every pole, window, and billboard seemed to have a picture of Kevin's freckled face plastered on it.

The mayor also approved printing enormous pictures of Kevin and posting them on the sides of city buses, so this was another effective way the kidnapping was publicized. She also offered a $5,000 reward from the city of San Francisco for information leading to Kevin's recovery.

Police entered Kevin's information as a missing person into the FBI's computer database a week after his disappearance. They also asked the California State Department of Justice to check out registered sex offenders, of which there were about 2,500 in the San Francisco Bay area alone. All along Kevin's parents had assumed that Kevin had been kidnapped by a sexual predator. They were just hoping that the person would eventually release Kevin unharmed.

Area newspapers covered the case daily. This helped keep Kevin's name and picture in the public eye. Some of the articles sought to educate the public about sexual predators. In one article, Denny Abbott of the Adam Walsh Child Resource Center advised that "Child stealers fall into no stereotype and may seem as ordinary as the guy next door." But, he said, "For the most part they're pedophiles, people who sexually use children."[7]

Lack of Physical Evidence

The investigation faced a huge stumbling block that it was never able to overcome. There was no physical evidence left at the bus stop where Kevin was last seen for police to investigate or that could give them any leads. Police inspector Richard Hesselroth commented, "Poof, yeah, he was there and then he's gone and nobody knows where he went. Somebody out there knows [what happened], but will that somebody ever tell us? Somebody does know the answer."[8]

This is often the case with kidnapped children who are never found. The physical evidence that could lead to the arrest and conviction of the criminal is at the location where the child is taken. Unless that location is found, it is extremely difficult to solve the case and bring the child safely home.

There have been many leads in the Kevin Collins case over the years and many suspects, including convicted child killer John Dunkel, whose three known victims resembled Kevin. There was also a report that suggested he was abducted by two Caucasian men who were driving a 1967 four-door royal blue Ford Galaxy. But none of the leads proved strong enough to result in an arrest.

Kevin Collins has never been found; his case remains open. Ten years after his abduction, his family members announced they believe he is dead. In a ceremony at a cemetery, they placed a marble bench with a photo of Kevin.

"I really think in my heart—I feel like probably—he was gone that first night, and I always pray it was fast,"[9] said Ann Collins.

Stranger Abductions

An abduction like the one that occurred with Kevin Collins is classified as a stranger kidnapping, or a stereotypical kidnapping. According to the Department of Justice, about 100 to 115 stranger kidnappings are reported

By the Numbers

20-39

Age range of males who commit most stranger abductions in the United States.

About 100 to 115 stranger kidnappings are reported each year in the United States, with the victim usually being a female under the age of fourteen.

each year in the United States. In many of the cases, there is some type of contact between the kidnapper and the victim before the kidnapping. Typically, the assault is sudden, ending with a quick abduction. Statistically, the victim is usually a female under the age of fourteen and is usually kept within 50 miles (80km) of the spot where she was abducted. Most of these kidnappings are carried out by unemployed white males who have a criminal record.

These types of kidnappings are extremely dangerous for the victim, both physically and psychologically. It is urgent that police respond to them as soon as possible. About 86 percent of the children involved in these incidents suffer physical and/or sexual assaults. More than 40 percent of them end with the child's death. In roughly 4 percent of the cases, the victim is never found.

Time is the enemy in kidnapping cases. Law enforcement authorities know this and work hard to quickly solve cases and rescue kidnapped victims.

CHAPTER 2

Finding the Victim

In kidnapping cases, statistics show that crimes are usually committed against the victim within the first three hours after the abduction. Because of this, law enforcement authorities know that it is vital to find the person as soon as possible, before the victim is harmed or killed. Investigators use many crime-solving techniques to try to locate kidnapped victims.

Kidnapped from Her Home

"Be quiet or I'll kill you."[10]

Nine-year-old Mary Katherine Smart heard those words on June 5, 2002, near Salt Lake City, Utah, in the darkness of the bedroom she shared with her fourteen-year-old sister, Elizabeth Smart. Mary Katherine pretended to be asleep but watched and listened as a stranger carrying what she believed was a gun ordered her sister to get out of bed and put on shoes. She heard her sister ask the man why he was doing this, and she thought he said "ransom" or "hostage."

The kidnapper's voice sounded familiar to her, but Mary Katherine could not pinpoint where or when she had heard it. She later described him as "soft-spoken." She never got a good look at the kidnapper's face, but this fact was initially kept a secret by the police during the investigation. When the kidnapper left the room with Elizabeth, Mary Katherine waited a minute and then followed them, almost running right into them because they had stopped in the hallway. Scared, she then ran back to her room and waited for almost two hours until she thought it was safe to run to her parents' bedroom to tell them what had happened.

Elizabeth Smart stands behind her younger sister Mary Katherine. Elizabeth was kidnapped from the girls' room in the middle of the night.

"I thought, you know, be quiet, because if he hears you, he might take you, too, and you're the only person who has seen this," Mary Katherine said later.[11]

Just before 4 A.M., Mary Katherine told her parents, Ed and Lois Smart, that a man with a gun had taken Elizabeth. Ed immediately jumped up and started searching the house. Still, it was not until Lois found that a downstairs window screen had been cut open that they realized Elizabeth really had been kidnapped.

Ed contacted the police at 4:01 A.M., and the police arrived twelve minutes later. He also called neighbors, family, and friends. The house was soon full of people trying to comfort the frightened family. A crowd is the last type of situation law enforcement authorities want at a crime scene. While it may seem unfeeling to try to prevent family and friends from coming in to help traumatized parents, having a lot of people walking around in the house can destroy crucial evidence and hurt the chances of finding the victim.

Ed later said, "By the time my brother David tried to get into our home, less than an hour after I called 911, the police wouldn't let him up because there were too many people in the house. The house had not yet been sealed as a crime scene, which was confusing and troubling to us. Looking back, this turned out to be a huge oversight on the part of the police. It wasn't until Sergeant Don Bell showed up that the house was finally secured at 6:54 A.M."[12]

Questioning the Family

At around 6:30 A.M., Ed and Lois and their older sons, Andrew and Charles, were taken to the police station for individual questioning. The police asked the parents what kind of girl Elizabeth was—did she have a boyfriend, did she take drugs, could she have run away, and what was her relationship like with them? They told the investigators that Elizabeth was a very young fourteen-year-old girl. She was an innocent girl who did not even use the Internet.

Elizabeth's parents, Lois and Ed, pleaded on the news for the return of their daughter.

Ed Smart was asked to take a polygraph test. When he later asked why this was necessary, Detective Jay Rhodes replied, "It's not uncommon for police to administer such tests to parents of missing children."[13]

Ed's brothers, Tom, Chris, and David, were also asked to take polygraphs. Tom's test stretched out to seven hours, compared to Ed's four-hour test, and was finally ruled inconclusive. He was also asked to write out his alibi so investigators could analyze it. All were eventually cleared.

Family members gave blood samples and had their fingerprints taken. They also filled out an FBI questionnaire that asked questions such as, "Did you kill Elizabeth? Who do you think could have taken her? If you had taken her, what would you have done?"

Mary Katherine was questioned twice that day. The first interview was informal, with Sergeant Don Bell, who would become the head of the task force for the case. He was assisted by a police department interview specialist. The second was a formal interview with only the specialist. Both investigators were careful not to push her too hard. Witnesses have been known to completely shut down after witnessing a traumatizing event and then being questioned too intensely. Mary Katherine stuck with the story she had given her parents earlier.

Story Is Withheld

While Elizabeth's family was being questioned at the police station, Ed Smart's brother Tom collected some recent photos of Elizabeth and loaded them onto his laptop. He was a photographer for the *Deseret News* in Salt Lake, and he had excellent media contacts. He then sent them to Chuck Wing, a photo editor at the *Deseret News*.

However, the police asked that the story and photos be held until they could verify that Elizabeth really had been kidnapped, that she was not just another teenager who had run away, and there was not some other domestic disturbance going on. That go-ahead was a long time coming, according to Tom Smart. "The police didn't give us the okay to go public with the story until more than three hours after the kidnapping."[14] After the OK was given, Wing immediately forwarded the digital pictures to every television station in Utah as well as to The Associated Press and Reuters News Service.

Hunt for Elizabeth Begins

Teams of bloodhounds were brought in that morning by the nonprofit group Intermountain K-9 Search & Rescue. They were given Elizabeth's clothing and pillowcases to sniff and then set loose to try to pick up the girl's scent. The dogs' handlers told the family that for best results, a search dog should get to an area before it becomes contaminated. However, by the time the dogs started searching, many people had already walked over the trails and hills behind the Smart home looking for Elizabeth. The dogs' search was not successful. One of the dogs did pick up Elizabeth's scent in a nearby gully, where she had jogged the night before she was kidnapped. It also picked up her scent on the side of her house that led to the backyard but lost it a few feet away.

FBI agent Mick Fennerty, Utah's lead Crimes Against Children representative, set up an Elizabeth Smart hotline and started checking on the Smarts' family finances, which was standard procedure in such situations. He also arranged for FBI profilers to come to the site. Meanwhile, police helicopters were brought in and hovered over the foothills, looking for Elizabeth and her captor. More local investigators were also brought in to work on the case. An initial search had found unidentified matching prints on the bedpost in Elizabeth's bedroom and the backdoor handle and a palm print on the window frame. Mary Katherine had described the kidnapper as white, about 5 feet 8 inches tall, with dark hair. She said he wore a tan, denim-type jacket and a white baseball cap. Police were hoping someone would recognize the kidnapper from the description that was being publicized on television, in newspapers, and on missing person flyers.

Police helicopters searched the hills behind the neighborhood where the Smarts lived looking for Elizabeth and her captor.

The police removed the Smarts' computers to check their hard drives. Some of the Smarts' neighbors were asked to go to the police station to be fingerprinted. That would help investigators identify prints found around the crime scene.

A massive volunteer search effort started the day after the kidnapping, working out of the newly formed Elizabeth Smart Search Center set up at the nearby Shriners Hospital. Representatives from the Laura Recovery Center had contacted Ed Smart upon learning of the kidnapping and offered their help organizing the search. About 1,200 volunteers divided up into groups of ten to twenty and searched the neighborhood and the rugged foothills nearby. At the same time, other searchers went door-to-door in an expanded search area, asking people whether they had seen or heard anything suspicious the night Elizabeth had been kidnapped or whether they had seen the person Mary Katherine had described.

By noon, dozens of the search groups had finished inspecting the zone they had been assigned and had marked suspicious areas or items with red tape. Possible leads were piling up. Sergeant David Craycroft went to the Elizabeth Smart Search Center at Shriners Hospital to work on them. He soon called for backup, and by day's end, three detectives were processing the leads full time. Few of the leads, however, turned out to be helpful.

Search Methodology Changes

Two FBI profilers developed a profile of the kidnapper, saying they believed this was a sex offense. They thought the crime was premeditated and that the kidnapper would have taken Elizabeth to a place he had carefully prepared. Further, they thought he had sexual issues and might have been arrested for previous sexual offenses.

This prompted police to track down and interview numerous ex-convicts. They sent many of the ones who had been charged with sex offenses back to jail on minor offenses unless they cooperated and talked to them about anyone they knew who might have committed the kidnapping.

To help publicize the kidnapping, *America's Most Wanted* television show aired a three-minute segment on the Elizabeth Smart case. "This beautiful girl was taken from her home at gunpoint by a kidnapper who went into the house through a window,"[15] host John Walsh said. Soon afterward, tips started coming in.

Police Target Suspects

As a result of the tips and possible leads, police officers interviewed hundreds of suspects. They also carefully looked at the people who had worked for the Smart family. For years the Smarts had hired homeless people to do odd jobs around their home. They thought it was a good way to help those less fortunate than themselves. Usually the people worked outside and never came into their home, but there were some exceptions. One of these people might have seen Elizabeth while he was working. In stranger kidnappings, the victim and the captor often make contact before the kidnapping takes place.

Finally, police zeroed in on 48-year-old handyman Richard Ricci, who was then in custody for a parole violation. Ricci had a long criminal history, including aggravated robbery, attempted homicide, and a prison escape. He had worked some odd jobs for the Smarts and was in and out of their home often. He had become familiar with their home and children. If he was guilty, that might explain how Elizabeth's abductor knew to exit through one of the few doors in the Smart home that was not hooked up to their alarm system. During the investigation, he confessed to stealing jewelry and other items from the Smarts. Ricci had been a suspect in other burglaries, including one that involved entering a dark bedroom where someone was sleeping, which police call a "thrill

Police Chief Rick Dinse answers questions at a news conference about the Smart kidnapping case. Police interviewed hundreds of people to gather information about the case.

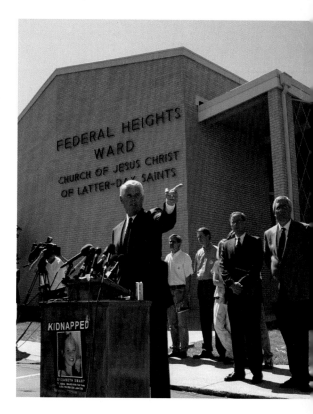

burglary." Thinking he was also responsible for Elizabeth's kidnapping, police focused their investigation on him

Ricci denied their claims. Then he died in jail on August 30 from a brain hemorrhage.

Sketch Artist

Partly because the investigation had stalled, well-known sketch artist Jeanne Boylan was brought in by authorities to interview Mary Katherine. Boylan had worked on several high-profile cases, including the Oklahoma City bombing. She had also created the hooded portrait of the Unabomber that helped the FBI identify Ted Kaczynski.

Renowned forensic scientist Dr. Henry Lee was brought in by the police when the Smart investigation stalled to see if he could offer any forensic insight into the case.

"Typically, I'm brought in to undo damage that's been done inadvertently by investigators through leading questions," Boylan said. "In this case, I was actually fairly stunned to arrive at the scene and find that none of the mistakes had been made. They've done exceptionally well at protecting and preserving Mary Katherine's recall."[16] Her praise, she said, was for both

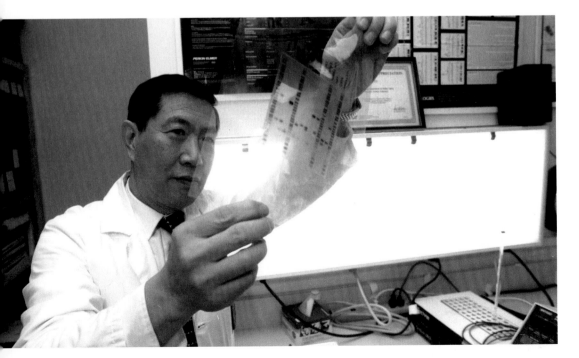

the Smart family and the investigators on the case.

Boylan later told the FBI and the police that she did not have enough information to make an effective sketch. She thought that if she worked with Mary Katherine to create a sketch, it might even be counterproductive because it might distort the girl's memory.

By the Numbers

203,900

Number of children abducted by family members every year.

World-Famous Forensic Evidence Expert

The Smarts wanted Dr. Henry Lee, a forensic scientist, to review their case to see whether he could come up with any additional insights. He had been successful in helping many other cases that had stalled. The police had initially refused but finally agreed to it if Lee was sworn to absolute confidentiality regarding his findings. That meant the Smarts would not have access to all the information Lee gave the police. However, new task force leader Cory Lyman did pass on some information to the Smarts.

He told them that Lee thought a man could have gotten into the house through the kitchen window by placing a chair outside it, stepping up on the chair and pushing his body through the cut screen. While the person would initially have to cut the screen from the outside, the person could then simply reach inside and cut the opening wider. This was contrary to what police investigators had thought. They did not think a man would have been able to squeeze through the window opening. They had suggested that the suspect had found another way in.

Afterward, Ed Smart questioned, "Why had it taken so long to bring in someone with the skills of Henry Lee?"[17]

Breakthrough

In October of 2002, Mary Katherine Smart suddenly remembered where she had heard the intruder's voice. She went to her parents and said, "I think I know who it is."[18] Lois Smart, along with the Smart children, had encountered "Immanuel" begging for money on a street corner and had offered him work. In November 2001, Immanuel worked for the Smart family for about five hours, working around the outside of their house. He told Ed Smart that he was a minister to the homeless. Mary Katherine said he was the one who broke into their room that night.

Police interviewed Mary Katherine about this new information. They did not think this was a trustworthy lead, however, because Mary Katherine had heard the man only whisper a few words that night in her bedroom after waking up from sleep. Police said there was no evidence that Immanuel was the kidnapper. This angered the Smarts, who believed the police should follow up on this possible lead.

The police suggested that the Smarts use the services of sketch artist Dalene Nelson to draw Immanuel's face from Ed's memory, as he had been with Immanuel longer than Mary Katherine. However, three months after the sketch was completed, the police were still urging the Smarts not to make it public, fearing its release would scare the kidnapper into hiding if he thought the police considered him a suspect.

By the Numbers

800,000

Number of missing children cases per year in the United States.

The sketch was finally publicized by John Walsh on *America's Most Wanted,* as well as on *Larry King Live.* However, when the Smarts knew him, Immanuel was clean-cut. Later, he grew thick, matted, long hair and a beard. So when the sketch was shown around Salt Lake City, no one recognized him.

Immanuel's sister, however, saw the sketch on television and called the police. She revealed that the 49-year-old's real name was Brian David Mitchell and also gave the police recent photos of him, which showed him with long hair. It would not be long before photos of Mitchell were widely distributed to the public.

Recovery

On March 12, 2003, Mitchell was spotted in Sandy, Utah, which was only a few miles away from Elizabeth's home in Salt Lake City. He was with two companions, a young girl and an older woman. Two people recognized him from the long-haired picture that was shown on *America's Most Wanted* and called police.

Sandy police chief Steve Chapman said the couple was evasive when questioned by police officers. The young girl, who was wearing a gray wig, sunglasses, and a veil, said her name was Augustine. But then she said, "I know who you think I am. You think I'm that girl who ran away, but I'm not." After police kept up their questioning, she finally said, "If thou sayest." Officer Victor Quezada said later he "took that as a yes."[19] A short time later Elizabeth Smart was reunited with her family. An investigation that cost an estimated $1.5 million and amassed 53,000 man-hours, with the police following up on more than 16,000 leads, was over.

Mitchell and his wife, Wanda Barzee, were arrested and charged with aggravated kidnapping, two counts of aggravated sexual assault, two counts of aggravated burglary, and conspiracy to commit kidnapping.

The FBI profile turned out to be accurate. After first seeing Elizabeth with her family on the street, then at her home the day he had worked there, Mitchell had stalked her while she jogged in her neighborhood. He then spent months preparing for the kidnapping, building a campsite in the foothills that blended into the trees and could not be seen from the air. It was only about 3 miles (5km) from the Smart home. Shortly after he kidnapped her, Mitchell conducted what he said was a marriage ceremony and made her his wife.

Ed Smart says Mitchell told Elizabeth that he would kill her and her family if she tried to flee or was not cooperative.

Brian Mitchell and his wife, Wanda Barzee, were arrested and charged with kidnapping, sexual assault, and burglary. Mitchell spent months preparing to kidnap Elizabeth Smart, who was found alive with him.

Technology to Recover Abducted Kids

Quickly transmitting a photo of an abducted child to law enforcement and media agencies can make a significant difference to an investigation. Gordon McNeil, FBI supervisory agent with the Child Abduction Unit said, "It's my opinion that if you do not recover that child within the first two to four hours, in all likelihood you are going to have a deceased child."

SocialTech, a nonprofit organization, was founded in 1994 to provide U.S. law enforcement agencies with the technology necessary to mount a fast, effective response to a missing or an abducted child. It used Technology to Recover Abducted Kids (TRAK), state-of-the art technology to transform relatively poor images, which may be all that are available in a crisis situation, into crisp, clear photographs that can be used to produce posters or flyers.

He says that people ask family members all the time why she did not try to escape—why she did not try to break free. He tells them that she did try, but she could not get away and that she was never left alone. "She went deep into hiding—for her own safety as well as for ours."[20]

One thing that really stands out about this case is that Elizabeth Smart is a very lucky person. Statistics show that most girls who are kidnapped like Elizabeth are murdered.

Eight Minutes in Texas

On January 12, 1996, nine-year-old Amber Hagerman; her mother; and her five-year old brother, Ricky, were visiting her grandparents at their home in Arlington, Texas. The children asked whether they could ride their bikes. Their mother and grandfather gave them permission to ride around the block once. After all, it was broad daylight along a main thoroughfare. The kids set off. Along the way, they stopped at an old parking lot where neighborhood kids liked to play on a ramp. They played for a while there too.

Not long afterward, Ricky returned alone to the house, saying that Amber was still playing at the ramp. The adults sent Ricky back to the lot to tell Amber to come right home.

A few minutes later Ricky hurried back, saying he could not find Amber. At that point Jimmie Whitson, Amber's grandfather, quickly drove to the parking lot, where he saw a police patrol car. The police officer told him that neighbor Jim Kevil had heard screaming. Kevil had quickly called 911 and reported the incident.

"I saw her riding up and down [the vacant lot]," he later said. "She was by herself. I saw this pickup. He pulled up, jumped out, and grabbed her … when she screamed, I figured the police ought to know about it, so I called them."[21]

By the time the officer arrived only minutes later, though, the truck had already sped away. Kevil was not close enough to get a good look at the kidnapper. He could only describe the man as white or Hispanic, and "not big, but very fast" and the fact that the vehicle was a black pickup truck.

Soon afterward, the girl's parents made a televised appeal, urging anyone with information to call police. A special hotline had been set up for this purpose. Local and national media representatives rushed to talk to them, as eager to get the story

Amber Hagerman's grandmother, Glenda Whitson, as well as several of Amber's family members went on the news to show pictures of Amber and spread the word about her kidnapping to as many people as possible.

41

as they were to get the story out to as many people as possible. That might be their only hope of getting their daughter back alive.

Body Found

Four days later a man walking his dog in north Arlington found Amber's body in a creek that had been swollen with heavy recent rain, about 8 miles (13km) away from where she had been kidnapped. Her throat had been slit. Investigators say that the nature of Amber's wounds suggested that the killer was inexperienced at that type of crime. They estimated that she had lived for about two days after her abduction. That meant there was a crime scene somewhere full of physical evidence, if only it could be found. As it was, finding her body in the creek made any forensic evidence extremely difficult to find.

Discovering the body of Amber Hagerman in a creek made any forensic evidence difficult to find. Investigators estimated that she lived only two days after her abduction.

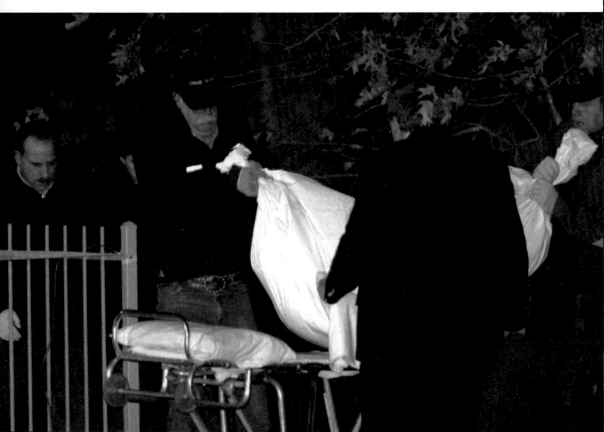

Amber's grandmother, Glenda Whitson, says the whole incident from the time Amber started off on her bike ride, until Kevil called 911 lasted only about eight minutes. "People have to know how fast these things can happen."[22]

She does not have much hope that the man who kidnapped Amber will ever be found. "They really don't have much to go on—a few fibers they found on the body, they tell us. They're still working on it, and they call us now and then. They say they'll never give up."[23]

Task Force

A special task force made up of police and FBI agents worked on the case over an eighteenth-month period at an estimated cost of more than $1 million. At the beginning of the case, the task force members practically worked nonstop, pausing only long enough to take brief naps. They eventually sifted through more than 5,000 leads. They also took more than a dozen false confessions. But they never found the killer. They say that having gotten away with one kidnapping and murder, the person might be encouraged to try it again. In fact, statistics show that he is probably planning to do just that, if he has not already done so.

Police Sergeant Mark Simpson headed the special task force in the Amber Hagerman case. He said, "There has never been any single person that we could look to and say he did it. … We're not done. This case is not finished, and it won't be until we make an arrest."[24]

AMBER Alerts

After Amber Hagerman's kidnapping and murder, a concerned citizen contacted a Dallas, Texas, radio station. He suggested that after a child has been kidnapped, when every minute counts, that area radio stations immediately send out bulletins about the kidnapping, similar to what they do when they broadcast severe weather warnings. The idea was then

The AMBER Alert system is a partnership between law enforcement agencies, broadcasters, and transportation agencies to activate an urgent bulletin in the most serious child-abduction cases. It has helped rescue more than 230 children nationwide.

discussed with general managers of radio stations in the Dallas area. They approved of it, saying that it was a public service and that it might help save the life of a child. The Dallas AMBER Alert program started in July of 1997. Although it was named after Amber Hagerman, it was dedicated to all children who had been kidnapped.

It has been described as a "voluntary partnership" between law enforcement agencies, broadcasters, and transportation agencies to activate an urgent bulletin in the most serious child-abduction cases. Broadcasters use the Emergency Alert System (EAS) to air a description and photo of the abducted child and any information available about the abductor, including description of the vehicle and the license plate number. The alert was established as a way to notify a community so people would be on the lookout for the child and/or abductor. The idea spread quickly, and by 2002, all fifty states had a statewide AMBER Alert in place, creating a nationwide network.

"AMBER Alert is a proven success and has helped rescue more than 230 children nationwide. More than 85 percent of those recoveries have occurred since AMBER Alert became a nationally coordinated effort in 2002,"[25] said Regina Schofield, assistant attorney general, Office of Justice Programs.

Parents Unhappy

Problems have developed with the AMBER Alert program. Different local and state jurisdictions often make conflicting decisions about when an alert should be issued. Some places have used AMBER Alerts when Alzheimer's patients have wandered off. Others restrict its use specifically for missing children.

Parents of missing children often plead that an AMBER alert be issued for their child. They question how anyone could

National Center for Missing and Exploited Children

The National Center for Missing and Exploited Children (NCMEC) is a private, nonprofit organization established in 1984. It works with parents, law enforcement agencies, communities, and others to help recover missing children and to raise awareness about ways to help prevent children from being kidnapped. It accepts tips and information from the public and distributes photos of missing children. It also coordinates its activities with law enforcement agencies, and works with numerous state and federal agencies.

When Gina DeJesus went missing, her parents requested an AMBER alert be issued but were told it could not be because the case did not meet the criteria (there was no description of a car or person). She was never found.

deny them the chance to reach a large number of people quickly to try to rescue their child. In cases where the missing person is later found dead, the grief-stricken parents are infuriated that the alert system was not used.

Usage Restricted

Law enforcement officials say they are careful to restrict the usage of AMBER Alerts, cautioning that if they are used too often, they will lose their effectiveness and people will stop paying special attention to them. This has become a highly charged emotional issue and sometimes leads to conflicts between law enforcers and a victim's parents.

"It has never been meant for missing children, lost children, or child-custody cases," according to Dee Anderson, the Fort Worth–area sheriff who helped initiate the first AMBER Plan in 1997. "Almost at times the plan is a victim of its own success,

What Are the Criteria for Issuing an Amber Alert?

What must law enforcement authorities do first?	Confirm that an abduction has taken place.
Is there an age limit for issuing an alert?	The child must be 17-years-old or younger.
What kind of description must be provided?	There must be a sufficient description of the child, captor or captor's vehicle before an Alert is issued.
What other criteria must be met?	The child must be determined to be at risk of serious injury or death.
Is there a national database where this information is entered?	AMBER Alert data is usually entered into the FBI's National Crime Information Center, with text describing the circumstances surrounding the abduction, and the case flagged as 'Child Abduction'.

Source: U.S. Department of Justice
Available online at: http://www.amberalert.gov/about/faqs.htm#question6

because now everyone wants it when a child is missing."[26]

When Gina DeJesus, age fourteen, went missing in Cleveland, Ohio, on a Friday in April 2004, her parents asked for an AMBER Alert. Her mother, Nancy Ruiz, said, "They told us we didn't meet the criteria because there was no description of a car or the person who abducted her."

For two days, Ruiz and Gina's father begged the Cleveland media and police to release a photo of the girl. Finally, TV stations aired DeJesus's photo that Sunday. "They say every second counts when a girl is abducted, and for 36 hours we got nothing. Whoever took my daughter got a 36-hour lead—and all because they wouldn't issue an AMBER Alert. He could have had her all the way to Canada by the time her picture was on TV."[27] As of 2007, Gina had not been found.

Law enforcement authorities are always looking for better ways to solve more crimes. They hope tools like AMBER Alerts, better crime scene management, and breakthroughs in technology will help them do that.

Hunting for a Kidnapper

Although the first priority in a kidnapping is to safely recover the victim, investigators also work to find and arrest the perpetrator. In the course of their investigation, they have to find evidence that will be acceptable, or admissible, in a court of law, to successfully convict the criminal. The first place they look is at the scene of the crime. Kidnapping cases are sometimes complicated by a lack of physical evidence present at the crime scenes. Especially in stranger abductions, which are often crimes of opportunity, and which happen quickly, few clues are left behind.

"The quality of the initial crime scene search can determine the outcome of the criminal investigation," according to retired New York Police Department police officer Vernon Geberth. "Do it right the first time. You only get one chance. Once things have been changed, once you lose that little window of opportunity, it's gone forever."[28]

Investigators consider the first twenty-four hours after a kidnapping the most crucial. The events will be fresh in the witnesses' minds, and the evidence will be in the best condition it will ever be in. The kidnapper's trail also will still be fresh.

Initial Call to the Crime Scene

Some parents have said they felt an overwhelming sense of confusion after their child was kidnapped. Most quickly call 911, but in a panic they also call family and friends. These people often instinctively rush to the home to offer comfort and help in the search. Although they mean well, they can inadvertently destroy fingerprints, footprints, or other evidence.

Therefore, investigators must restrict people, despite their protests, from a kidnapping site.

When police officers arrive, they secure the crime scene. They close off the area with crime scene tape and establish a single route in and out. The only people who can enter the area are those actively engaged in processing the scene. It is common knowledge among law enforcement officials that the more people there are in a crime scene, the greater are the chances that evidence can be lost, contaminated, or even stolen. Criminals have been known to return to the scene of their crime to try to steal or destroy evidence that could be traced to them. The police are well aware of the importance of preserving physical evidence for the crime scene investigators and will stop unauthorized visitors from entering the area.

If a crime scene is not secured with crime scene tape by investigators, important fingerprints, footprints, or other evidence can be accidentally destroyed.

Some jurisdictions keep a log of everyone who enters the scene, including the time the person enters and leaves and whether the person removes anything. This information can later be used at a trial to prove there was no evidence tampering. Investigators may also photograph the soles of the shoes of anyone who enters the scene, so footprints made by investigators can be differentiated from those of possible suspects.

Jarrett Hallcox and Amy Welch teach crime scene investigators at the National Forensic Academy that there are eight steps to working a crime scene:

1. Approach the scene.
2. Secure and protect the scene.
3. Conduct a preliminary survey.
4. Photograph the scene.
5. Sketch a diagram of the scene.
6. Perform a detailed search for evidence.
7. Collect the evidence.
8. Conduct the final survey.

Every Contact Leaves a Trace

Investigators use Locard's Exchange Principle as the theory behind their work. Dr. Edmond Locard (1877–1966) established one of the first forensic laboratories in the world in Lyons, France, in 1910. He believed that "every contact leaves a trace"; that there was a cross transference of small traces between the perpetrator and the victim. He proved this principle when he investigated the case of Emile Gourbin, who was accused of strangling a woman. Gourbin had an alibi, but Locard scraped beneath the man's fingernails and found flakes of skin coated with powder from the dead woman's face. Gourbin later confessed to the crime.

Beginning the Investigation

According to one forensic investigator, "When I get sent to a scene, I'll do a walk-through to see what I'm dealing with. My observations usually start on the outside, mainly because one of your main objectives when you're processing a scene is to identify fragile evidence and take steps to protect it, document and collect that first, so anything outdoors, obviously, has the potential to be more fragile than evidence indoors because of the weather and everything else."[29]

Evidence response teams intensively document a crime scene and carefully collect as much evidence as they can find.

When investigators reach the place where the kidnapping occurred, they take notes as they interview the police officers who arrived initially, in order to fully document the crime scene. The first responders can tell investigators about any short-lived evidence, such as odors that have since dissipated, and other first impressions of the scene that may be of value to the case. Investigators usually write detailed notes, because a case can sometimes take years before going to trial. When that time comes, the investigator's notes will have to be sufficient to jog his or her memory.

If there are any witnesses, they will be kept apart and interviewed separately. This is done so that one person's view of what happened does not influence anyone else's story. Interviews are also done this way so that if a suspect is caught and tried, defense lawyers will have less of a chance to cast doubt on one witness's story, if it is backed up by another witness.

Searching for Evidence

The way a crime scene is searched usually depends on the nature of the area itself. While indoor crime scenes are in a contained area, outdoor crime scenes can pose a challenge. If it is a large open area such as a park or field, investigators may line up and walk forward together, so they do not overlook anything.

Crime Labs

After evidence has been gathered, it is brought to a crime laboratory, where it is tested with sophisticated instruments to try to determine the person or persons who committed the crime.

"We've had doors in here. Garbage cans. Car bumpers and fenders for hit-and-runs. Mattresses, back seats of cars for rape cases. Lamps, arrows, fans—we get them all in here; they're used as weapons," said officer Jim Doran, head of the Criminalistics Sections of the crime lab at the Chicago Police Department. "We get everything in here you can kill a person with."

Not all labs are alike. Small labs might have just one scientist and analyze only basic evidence. They send anything that requires sophisticated analysis to a central lab. There, multiskilled technicians do a wide variety of tasks, or there may be specialist scientists who each focus on a complex field.

This type of search is hard to do if the kidnapping takes place in a small town with a small investigative force. In that case, additional law enforcement personnel may have to be called in from nearby areas to help.

One investigator said of finding evidence, "The whole premise of crime scene investigation is that anytime one person comes in contact with something else, they are going to leave some trace of themselves, or pick up a trace of the other material. There is always going to be this transfer of material. You just have to look."[30]

Photographing the Crime Scene

After the initial walk-through of the kidnapping crime scene, one of the first things to be done is the crime scene photographers take photos. All evidence has to be documented and photographed before it can be moved to a forensic laboratory for further analysis. Although kidnapping cases require urgency, investigators must still be thorough and not overlook anything.

"There is nothing more important in crime scene investigation than photography. When arriving at a crime scene, it is imperative to begin taking photographs as soon as possible before anything in the scene is disturbed—and to take as many as possible thereafter. Crime scene pho-

Crime scene photographers take as many photos as possible since photographs will be the main documentation that investigators refer to after leaving the crime scene.

tographs will be the main documentation to refer to once everyone has left the scene, and they just might be the only piece of evidence a jury sees," [31] according to National Forensic Academy instructor Jarrett Hallcox. Typical photographs taken at a kidnapping crime scene include those of blood spattering or stains and prints of fingers, shoes, or tire impressions.

While every photographer has his or her own technique, Kansas Bureau of Investigation (KBI) agent Harold Nye's advice to crime scene photographers is to, "Shoot your way in and shoot your way out. Never go into a room before you take a picture. As you leave the scene, repeat the picture-taking in reverse order." [32] Ideally, using Nye's method, nothing will be missed.

When arriving at a kidnapping crime scene, most photographers will walk around to get an idea of what pictures they will need to take. As they do this, they are extremely careful not to disturb anything, to avoid contaminating evidence. They also check with the investigators to see what they want photographed in greater detail. This could be something the investigators think may turn out to be an important piece of evidence in the kidnapping investigation.

Each crime scene is unique and has its own requirements, but there are some things that forensic photographers do at every crime scene. They need to take a series of pictures that will provide a look of as much of the crime scene as possible. Nothing is moved; everything is photographed in situ (in place). The photos enable people who were not there to get a clear idea of what the crime scene looked like.

"I make up a kind of mental list as I go along. Sometimes, especially if it's a more involved scene, I'll write down some notes about what I'm seeing and ideas for processing. I start with the documentation process. Then I start photographing the scene from the outside to the point of entry through to the crime scene itself. Still photographs for the majority of scenes, sometimes video for homicide cases. You get a feel for the scene before you start collecting anything," [33] according to one crime scene photographer.

Photographers generally use the "four corners" method to record indoor scenes. First, a series of photos is taken from the doorway of the room from which the victim was abducted. Then the photographer moves to the three remaining corners of the room in turn, to show the crime scene from different angles. The photographer also takes pictures of all entrances to the crime scene.

Some items need to be photographed close-up, so that certain details are enhanced and revealed. These include things either that seem to be out of place or that do not belong. They might have been moved or left by the kidnapper, so they will be checked for fingerprints.

To make hard-to-see evidence visible, photographers may use forensic lamps equipped with changeable colored filters to direct brilliant narrow beams at the evidence. For example, ultraviolet light makes fingerprints and some stains glow.

Photographers are careful to document and describe what they are photographing in a logbook, so they can keep track of each shot. They include

Items at a crime scene are often marked with an evidence marker and photographed close-up to enhance certain details.

not only the details of what is in each photo but also the time, date, location, and the processing procedure. Also in their photos they will include something to give an idea of the scale, or size. This could be as simple as a 6-inch (15cm) ruler or a measuring tape.

Chief forensic photographer Marty Coyne says his work schedule is unpredictable. He has to be prepared to be called to work at any time. He says it is a "24-hour, seven-day-a-week job."[34]

The most widely used technique for fingerprint collection is dusting, which makes latent fingerprints more visible.

Fingerprints

While the photographer shoots pictures, other investigators search for fingerprints. "Fingerprint collection is the cornerstone of crime scene investigation,"[35] according to Jarrett Hallcox. Finding a suspect's fingerprints enables investigators to check databases of known criminals to try to find a match. Places where the kidnapper might have gotten in, such as windows and doors, are checked first.

Each person's fingerprints are unique. Even the prints of identical twins are different; they can be distinguished from one another by their ridges. Secretions from the sweat glands line these ridges and leave telltale traces on things people touch. "Whatever you touch you're going to transfer moisture, especially if you're emotional in the commission of a crime,"[36] said one evidence technician.

The most widely used technique for fingerprint collection is dusting. This is effective on nonporous surfaces. Soft brushes are used to apply powder to a surface that the kidnapper might have touched. The powder adheres to the moist lines left by the skin ridges. After it has been powdered, the print can then be "lifted" using low-tack adhesive tape. The print is then placed on a card and preserved as evidence.

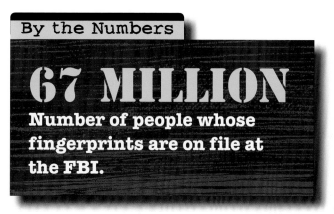

By the Numbers

67 MILLION
Number of people whose fingerprints are on file at the FBI.

For prints on porous surfaces, such as paper, dusting will not work. In these cases, investigators use chemical reagents such as ninhydrin and DFO. These react with the proteins present in sweat. The surface is either sprayed with or dipped in the solution, then carefully warmed. Ninhydrin-treated prints turn purple, and DFO makes fingerprints glow when they are lit by laser or blue-green light.

"How you touch objects is crucial," advises one print specialist. "I always tell detectives: When you're collecting evidence from the scene, and you know how a person would usually pick up an object—like picking up a wineglass by its stem, say—then pick it up in a totally different way, so you're not going to touch any prints. And secure it in a box, so the whole surface is protected and isn't going to move."[37]

Manhunt in England

Fingerprint evidence has long helped investigators solve kidnapping cases. In May 1948, three-day-old June Devaney was kidnapped from her hospital crib in Blackburn, England. After a two-hour search, police found her battered corpse nearby. This incident launched one of the biggest manhunts in British history.

Fingerprints were found on a hospital bottle that did not match those of hospital staff or any known criminals, so police fingerprinted every male voter in Blackburn—more than 40,000 people. However, none of the prints matched those on the bottle. Desperate to find the killer, police checked ration cards, which people in England needed to buy food during and right after World War II.

They found that 200 Blackburn men were not registered voters. Police promptly took fingerprints from these men, and found one set that matched those on the bottle. Confronted with this evidence, twenty-two-year-old former soldier Peter Griffiths confessed. He was later convicted and hanged.

Automated Fingerprint Identification System

Today, law enforcement officers have extensive database records of fingerprints. This has revolutionized fingerprint searches. While it once took weeks of searching to find a fingerprint match, now it takes only minutes to find a match. The Automated Fingerprint Identification System (AFIS) is a national fingerprint and criminal history system maintained by the FBI's Criminal Justice Information Services (CJIS) division. It provides automated fingerprint capability, electronic image storage, and electronic exchange of fingerprints and re-

The Automated Fingerprint Identification System (AFIS) is a national fingerprint and criminal history system that is functional 24 hours a day, 365 days a year.

sponses 24 hours a day, 365 days a year.

Palm Prints

Along with fingerprints, palm prints have started to play an important part in kidnapping investigations. The Automated Palmprint Identification System (APIS) has a database that houses palm prints of known criminals. People who use the system say that though criminals may be careful about not leaving fingerprints, some are not aware of this new identification system and are caught after leaving palm prints at the scene. For example, there are two places in particular outside a house where investigators might find palm prints. Sometimes a kidnapper unscrews an exposed lightbulb on the outside of a house before breaking in. A kidnapper who does this rests the outside palm, or "karate chop" side, of the hand against the side or base of the lightbulb. Also, if the kidnapper tries to peer into a window, again it's common to rest the outside palm against the glass. Prints can be obtained from these surfaces.

Surprising Discovery About Children's Fingerprints

When Art Bohanan was an investigator with the Knoxville, Tennessee, Police Department, he worked on a kidnapping/ murder case of a three-year-old girl in 1993. The prime suspect claimed he was innocent, but witnesses said they had seen the child in the man's car. When Bohanan processed the inside of the car for fingerprint evidence, however, the only prints he could find were those of the suspect. He wondered what happened to the little girl's prints, which he expected to find there.

He started researching the length of time a child's fingerprints will last and was amazed by what he learned. Scientists at the Oak

By the Numbers

5 TO 10

Number of evidence items state crime labs process per case.

Investigators depend heavily on the analysis of DNA to convict kidnappers.

Ridge National Laboratory confirmed that children's prints don't last very long, because their sweat glands have not fully developed. Until the age of puberty, a child's prints evaporate quicker than those of adults, simply because their prints are made up mostly of water. Research is currently under way to develop methods of enhancing the capabilities of lifting children's fingerprints.

DNA Identifies Suspects

To get evidence that will convict kidnappers, investigators depend heavily on the analysis of deoxyribonucleic acid (DNA), the genetic material found in cells. This has become an important weapon for forensic investigation. DNA is found in the cells of all living things. Its long double-helix-shaped strands contain information that is unique to each person.

The way DNA is collected, preserved, and tested is critical to the outcome in criminal prosecutions by either helping to convict the guilty or exonerate the innocent. Scientists can take DNA from substances such as blood, hair, or skin to make a DNA fingerprint, which can be used to match that of a victim or perpetrator. Scientists and investigators can have positive proof that a suspect was at a crime scene if they can match DNA found at the scene with the suspect's DNA.

Dog DNA Helps Solve Case

Usually human DNA is analyzed in investigations, but that is not always the case. On Saturday, February 2, 2002, when Brenda Van Dam went to wake up her seven-year-old daughter, she found that Danielle was missing. Her husband remembered waking up in the middle of the night to let their dog out of their suburban San Diego, California, home. He had noticed a sliding door was open, but at the time, he had not thought much about it. Now, the parents quickly called the police. Police officers responded; some interviewed neighbors, others searched the area, and crime scene analysts started processing the family home.

Suspicion soon fell on neighbor David Westerfield, after police said he acted nervous during a routine interview a few days after the kidnapping. "Mr. Westerfield was sweating profusely under both armpits to the point the sweat rings were protruding out from his armpits several inches,"[38] officer Johnny Keene said.

Police also thought it was suspicious that Westerfield had left on a road trip the morning that Danielle went missing. He told investigators he had driven to the desert, then the beach, and then headed home. Then he had changed his mind and driven to the mountains and then

Seven-year-old Danielle Van Dam was kidnapped from her home in the middle of the night on February 1, 2002.

back to the desert. Keene said Westerfield described thirteen destinations in all. Westerfield later accompanied investigators and retraced the route he had taken.

After getting a search warrant, police searched his home and RV and found evidence including fingerprints, fibers, hair, and blood linking Westerfield to Danielle.

Caught in a Lie

DNA tests revealed that the hair came from a Weimaraner. This was considered significant because Danielle had been playing and wrestling around with the family dog, a Weimaraner, before she went to bed. This and other evidence was used to establish the fact that Danielle was inside Westerfield's RV at some point. Westerfield had previously told police he was driving around in his RV at the time that she had disappeared. Caught in a lie, he was arrested.

Danielle Van Dam's body was found in east San Diego on February 27 by a team of volunteers. The site was along the driving route that Westerfield told police he had taken in his RV. Forensic dentist Norman Sperber identified the body through Danielle's dental records. Cause of death could not be determined because of the body's state of advanced decomposition.

Westerfield was found guilty of kidnapping and murder and sentenced to death. As of 2007 he was awaiting execution.

"There are three things that really make a case. It is evidence that proves whether a crime has been committed; it is evidence that proves whether a particular suspect committed a crime; and it is evidence that exonerates the innocent,"[39] according to crime scene investigator trainer Hallcox.

Sometimes when there is a lack of physical evidence or local investigators feel they need additional assistance, they call in experts, such as FBI special agents. They may have the additional training or resources necessary to crack a particularly puzzling case.

Based on DNA evidence from fingerprints, hair, and blood found in David Westerfield's (sitting) home and RV, he was found guilty of kidnapping and murder and sentenced to death.

CHAPTER 4

Profiling Kidnappers

Profiling is a technique used by law enforcement authorities to help solve crimes by studying a criminal's behavior to learn what type of person would have committed a particular crime. Though it cannot pinpoint the guilty person, it can help investigators eliminate subjects and narrow their search. Profilers are often called in to help when leads have dried up, and local authorities have not identified a prime suspect.

Early Profiling

In the 1970s, FBI special agent Howard "Bud" Teten was an instructor at the FBI National Academy at Quantico, Virginia. Previously he had been a police officer and crime scene specialist. He thought that law enforcement up until then had ignored teaching the psychology of criminal behavior, so he added profiling as part of his applied criminology class.

Teten talked about the importance of analyzing the behaviors and traits of criminals and what factors contribute or lead them to commit certain types of crimes. He believed if investigators did this they could make deductions and predict the characteristics of the individual who committed the crime, which in turn would help solve the case. At the time, this was a revolutionary concept. Teten wrote up the first official FBI profile and is generally regarded as the father of modern criminal profiling.

Behavioral Science Unit

In 1972, the FBI started its Behavioral Science Unit (BSU). The group initially had eleven agents, all of whom had shown skill at behavioral analysis. Though the agents were taught a variety of techniques to help them solve criminal cases, profiling became the cornerstone of their methodology. They developed into an elite law enforcement group. So many requests for their resources came in from around the United States that they eventually trained other agents to help teach the program. These eleven agents also went out to local jurisdictions to teach. When doing this, they managed to help solve some complex cases. This increased the visibility of the profiling program.

In the 1970s the FBI's National Academy at Quantico, Virginia, began to emphasize the importance of analyzing the behaviors and traits of criminals to make deductions about individuals who committed certain crimes.

16-week Profiling Program

When FBI agents are selected to participate in a profiling program, they go through a 16-week classroom-based program. The course work includes the following subjects:

basic psychology
criminal psychology
forensic science
body recovery
criminal investigative analysis
death investigation
threat assessment
crimes against children
sexual victimization of children/Internet issues
interview and interrogation procedures

Profiling Identifies Suspect in Montana

One such puzzling case occurred in Montana in 1973–74 and involved seven-year-old Susan Jaeger, who had been kidnapped from her tent while on a family camping trip. The investigation had slowed because no physical evidence had been found that could offer any leads. Profilers developed a psychological profile, saying the suspect was a young, white male who killed for sexual gratification and might have kept body parts of victims as souvenirs. They believed this pointed to possible suspect David Meirhofer. Local police, however, thought the profilers were wrong. Meirhofer was well groomed, was well educated, and had passed a polygraph. But the profilers remained convinced that Meirhofer was guilty.

Meirhofer was later arrested and found guilty of murdering a young woman in 1974. At first he refused to say anything about Susan Jaeger, but eventually he admitted that he had kidnapped Susan and kept her imprisoned for a period of time before killing her. He also confessed to murdering two boys. A few hours after confessing, he committed suicide in jail. The profile turned out to be accurate.

The profilers went to assist only in cases that they were invited to help in or that clearly involved federal crimes. They found that many jurisdictions were eager to work with experienced agents who had seen many crimes and crime scenes. Many of the smaller towns they went to had had little or no major crime cases.

However, some law enforcement agencies resisted change and did not trust this new technique. They were used to dealing only with hard evidence they could see and touch. The profilers were trying to evaluate the indirect results of clever criminal minds. It was a totally different way to go about solving crimes.

Interviewing Prisoners to Improve Profiles

FBI special agents John Douglas, Richard Ault, and Robert Ressler believed that they might learn things that would help them solve crimes if they talked to criminals in prison. They could learn more about criminals such as why they had committed their crimes, why they chose certain people instead of others to be their victims, and why they had carried out their crimes in the manner they had.

"We were talking about these cases as part of our instruction," said former FBI special agent John Douglas. "So I figured, why not see if they'll talk to us."[40]

Soon after they started interviewing the convicts, they modified their techniques, narrowing their focus to try to get more specific information that would help them form patterns for their predictions about crimes and criminals. They thought

FBI Special Agents believed that interviewing criminals in prison, such as domestic terrorist Ted Kaczynski, would help them learn more about why these people committed crimes and why they chose certain victims instead of others. All of this gathered information helped agents create profiles of certain criminal types.

their professional experience, coupled with the knowledge they were gathering would help them determine the age range, mental condition, and probable employment status of offenders. Using this methodology, they could help investigators narrow their suspect list, and point to a particular suspect.

"Profiling is an aid—just one tool among many," writes forensic psychologist Katherine Ramsland in *The Criminal Mind*. "The fact is, most cases are cracked through detailed police work."[41]

A Kidnapping Ends in Murder

Profiling can be an effective technique to focus an investigation when traditional investigative methods haven't worked, as in the case of Mary Frances Stoner. In December of 1979, 12-year-old Mary was kidnapped 100 yards (91m) from her front door after getting off a school bus in Adairsville, Georgia. Her body was found a few days later in some woods about 10 miles (16km) away. She had been raped, strangled, and killed by blows to her head with a rock, which was found near her body.

After police could not come up with any leads, an FBI agent in Georgia called FBI profiler John Douglas and asked for assistance. Douglas was called in to help them determine what type of person might have committed the murder. "I use a formula," Douglas said. "How plus Why equals Who. If we can answer the hows and whys in a crime, we generally can come up with the solution."[42]

Unknown Subject Profiled

Douglas was given descriptions of the crime scene, autopsy results, and information about Mary's personality. Douglas believes it is crucial to learn significant facts about the victim and develop what he calls a "detailed victimology," important facts about the victim's life, especially in the days and hours right before the abduction or murder. Some profilers even draw up a time line, to map the victim's movements. They try to determine where the victim and the criminal might have crossed paths. After analyzing the evidence in the case, Douglas concluded that, among other things, the unknown subject probably lived in the area and knew that the spot where he took the girl was secluded and he could safely take her there without being seen. Douglas also believed the suspect had killed the girl to prevent her from identifying him, which was another clue that the man was a local resident.

Profile Points to Suspect

When police looked at the profile, it seemed to describe Darrell Devier, someone they had already interviewed as a possible suspect. Devier had been trimming trees close to the Stoner home on the day Mary had been kidnapped. He had also been accused previously of raping a 13-year-old girl, but the case had been dropped due to insufficient evidence. Douglas believed Devier kidnapped Mary right after she got off the bus and forced her into his car and raped her there. He surmised that Mary probably started struggling and crying, and that destroyed

FBI profiler John Douglas was brought in by police to create the correct setting for the interrogation of kidnapping and murder suspect Darrell Devier. Douglas knew the perfect balance of stressors that would get Devier to confess.

the sexual fantasy Devier had had about the rape, so he took her into the woods and strangled her. When she did not die right away, he beat her head repeatedly with a fifty-pound rock until she did.

When confronted by detectives, Devier strenuously denied the accusations. He was given a polygraph test, but the results were inconclusive. At that point, from Devier's attitude, actions, and words, it appeared to Douglas that Devier thought he could get away with the crime by being "uncooperative, cocky, and elusive."

From experience, Douglas knew that months of work on a case could be lost if just one interrogation is conducted without careful preparation. While profilers sometimes conduct interrogations, most often their job is to prepare investigators from local law enforcement or from state or federal agencies to effectively question a suspect. So he helped the interrogators formulate an approach that would zero in on the suspect's weakness, which is a strategy he believes usually gets positive results.

Setting the Stage for Successful Interrogation

First, a team made up of FBI agents and local police officers would conduct the interview. Having Devier walk into a room and see all the law enforcement personnel there would impress upon him the fact that this was an important interview, and that he was their prime suspect.

The questioning would take place at night in a room with dim lighting. This would put him in a relaxed mood. Then, a stressor, something from the murder, would be brought in. This would abruptly surprise him, and he would be caught off guard, which would make him vulnerable.

Stacks of bulging file folders with his name on them would be brought in and placed around the room. Although some of them might only be filled with blank paper, Devier would not know that. Law enforcement officials hoped he would think they had built up a strong case against him.

Then the investigators decided to try to rattle Devier to get a reaction from him. They brought the bloodstained rock that had been used to kill Mary Stoner into the interrogation room. When he saw the rock, Devier began sweating and breathing heavily. Douglas had anticipated Devier would act that way if he was guilty. Douglas knew from investigating other blunt-force trauma cases that Devier would have gotten blood all over his clothing and hands when he killed Mary. Seeing the rock again would bring back all the emotion Devier had felt when he had beaten her to death. After further questioning Devier confessed not only to Mary's kidnapping, rape, and murder but also to another rape. He was later convicted of Mary Stoner's murder and was executed in 1995.

Robert Hansen admitted to killing 17 women over ten years and disposing of their bodies in Alaska after psychological profiling was used to get search warrants on his property.

Profiling Gives Insight on Tough Case

Another kidnapping case in which profiling helped law enforcement officials began on June 30, 1982. A police officer at Anchorage Airport in Alaska encountered a woman who claimed she had been kidnapped at gunpoint, taken to a cabin in the woods, and raped. She escaped while her attacker was loading his airplane.

After the woman described her kidnapper, the description matched that of local businessman and hunter Robert Hansen. She was also

able to identify his house as well as his distinctive airplane, a blue and white Piper Super Cub.

Hansen denied her accusation and said he had never seen her before. Two of his business associates gave him an alibi. However, the police remained suspicious. They had discovered the bodies of two women in 1980 in the wilderness. Then, in September of 1982, the body of another woman was discovered in a remote Alaskan region. She had been killed by a high-powered rifle. A year later the body of another woman was found in the same area. The police believed that Hansen was the man responsible for the murders, but they needed help to prove it, so they contacted the FBI. The FBI's Investigative Support Unit assigned profiler John Douglas to the case.

Douglas studied the case information and learned that Hansen had a socially isolated childhood and a strict, overbearing father. Physically, he was short, had severe acne, and spoke with a stammer. Douglas thought that because of these things, Hansen was probably teased a lot by his peers and might have had trouble with girls as a teenager. The murders might have been his way of venting his anger against women. Douglas also thought that Hansen specifically chose prostitutes as his victims because many of them moved often and most did not have families, so they would not easily be missed by friends or family.

Douglas thought that Hansen was probably using his plane to dump the bodies in remote spots, where they would be hard to find. Chances also were good that he had started releasing his victims in the wilderness, and then hunting them down like animals. The profiler felt it was also possible that because Hansen was a hunter, he might have kept items from the women as souvenirs, or trophies. Finding these items would give

By the Numbers

8 OUT OF 10

Number of stranger kidnapping victims in the United States who are white females.

authorities the evidence they needed to prove Hansen's guilt.

Police Stick with the Suspect

Douglas felt they had to find a way to break Hansen's alibi. He strongly suspected that Hansen's friends were lying for him, so he encouraged local authorities to threaten the men with being brought up on charges of lying to law enforcement officials.

State police sergeant Glenn Flothe took Douglas's advice and brought in the men for questioning. When confronted, both men confessed they had previously lied and were not with Hansen the night the young prostitute was kidnapped. After continued questioning, they also confided that Hansen was committing insurance fraud. He had claimed a number of items had been stolen and had collected $13,000 from an insurance company for the loss but actually had the items hidden in his basement.

Profilers helped solve the 1992 kidnapping case of Sidney Reso, president of Exxon International.

At this point, police officers raided Hansen's home. They found a hidden storage space in the rafters of his attic. There, they found jewelry and ID cards taken from the victims, as well as a map marked with the locations of the bodies. There were also some guns, including a rifle. Ballistics tests run on the rifle matched the guns that had killed two of the women. Confronted with this evidence, Hansen finally confessed. He was later convicted, and sentenced to 499 years in prison. This case set a legal precedent in 1983 when psychological profiling was used when issuing search warrants on Hansen's property.

"Sometimes [profilers] can go a long way in determining the identity of an unknown offender. Sometimes we can only say who it is not, from a behavioral standpoint,"[43] Douglas said.

Profiling Helps Solve Ransom Case

Profilers helped solve another kidnapping case that began on April 29, 1992, when Sidney Reso, president of Exxon International, was kidnapped as he left his home in New Jersey. A ransom note directed the FBI to set up a cell phone number that could be used in negotiations and to wait for further instructions. The note claimed the kidnappers were environmental activists who disagreed with Exxon's corporate practices. A man and a woman later called and also delivered more notes, ultimately demanding $18.5 million.

An FBI profiler studied the ransom notes. Because of the way the notes were worded, he thought it was likely that the writer had a security background and also had some previous connection to either Reso or Exxon. Whoever had done it had obviously carefully planned the way Reso would be kidnapped, finding out where he lived, his daily routine, and when would be the best time for a kidnapping attempt. However, other things, such as the kidnappers' reliance on cell phones suggested a lack of criminal experience. A more experienced criminal probably would have realized that cell phone calls can be traced. The profiler also thought the kidnappers were not really environmentalists; they had simply kidnapped Reso to get a large sum of money, thinking that Exxon would pay the money to have their executive safely released.

Kidnappers Traced

Negotiations with the kidnappers dragged on for seven weeks, during which time the kidnappers sent a number of ransom notes and made fourteen calls to authorities. The kidnappers assured them that Reso was still alive and well. More than 300 law enforcement investigators were brought in to work on the case, including FBI agents, city police, state police, and canine units, among others. Statistically, the longer the investigation remained unsolved, the slimmer the chances were of finding Reso alive.

Kidnapper Irene Seale led authorities to Sidney Reso's body in exchange for a reduced sentence.

Meanwhile, one of the calls was traced to a pay phone, which the FBI put under surveillance. Arthur Seale was seen making one of the calls. When Arthur was later spotted driving a rental car, the FBI followed him, hoping he would lead them to Reso. When it turned out he was returning the car to the rental agency, where he was met by his wife, Irene Seale, known as Jackie, they arrested them both. A search of the car revealed a pair of latex gloves identical to the ones that Arthur Seale had been seen wearing while at the pay phone. They also found a few .38 caliber bullets and a 1985 Exxon directory that listed Sidney Reso's home address.

The profile turned out to be accurate. Arthur Seale was a former police officer who had worked for Exxon as a security expert, helping Exxon develop ways to deal with executive kidnappings. He was aware of the fact that, years earlier, Exxon had paid $15 million in ransom for one of its executives in South America. Arthur had substantial business debts and had come up with the kidnapping plan as a way to get a large amount of money.

At first, Arthur and Jackie Seale refused to cooperate with police. Finally, Jackie agreed to help in exchange for a reduced sentence. She led authorities to where Reso was buried. She said that he died from a heart attack and that they had never meant to hurt him. However, prosecutors painted a very different picture of the way the Seales had treated Reso. Arthur Seale had pulled out his handgun while kidnapping a struggling Reso and had accidentally wounded him in the arm. Then he tied up Reso and made him lie in a coffin-shaped box. Reso was kept there, in temperatures that heated up to over a hundred degrees. He was only periodically given water, Tylenol, and sleeping pills to ease the pain for his untreated wound. He had heart problems, and four days later, he died of a heart attack. After he died, the Seales took the box with Reso's corpse to a remote section of Bass River State Forest, where it lay undiscovered for almost two months.

Arthur Seale received a life sentence for murder, kidnapping, and extortion. Jackie Seale was sentenced to twenty years

Making Prints Visible on Tape

Criminals use black electrical tape to help make bombs, use shipping tape to mail anthrax, and tie up people with duct tape. They often just discard the tape, not thinking of it as evidence that can be processed. Crime scene investigators are interested in the sticky side of tape, because it can pull dead skin off the fingers.

Scientists at the Michigan State Crime Lab developed a substance that allows investigators to lift prints off tape. It also works on latex gloves, allowing investigators to find prints on the inside of the gloves.

for extortion.

Profiling Consultants

FBI agents are not the only profilers. Forensic scientist Dean Widnman consults on as many as a hundred crimes a year, ten to fifteen of which require offender profiling. He says he might be contacted by any number of sources, such as victims' families, law enforcement agencies, lawyers, or others about criminal cases that seem to have gone cold, with no leads or suspects. Some of the cases might be months old, and others may be years old.

When he starts to work on a case, he receives information such as the crime scene notes and sketches, forensic photos, police reports, crime lab reports, and statements from family members. Every case is unique and requires its own investigative approach. He interviews police officers, victims' families, and the forensic scientists who were involved in the case.

He also visits the crime scene, which he finds particu-

Becoming an FBI Special Agent

Job Description:

FBI special agents are recruited from a wide variety of educational disciplines and professions. In addition to conducting investigations and protecting the United States from foreign intelligence and terrorist threats, FBI special agents also provide leadership and assistance to law enforcement agencies.

Education:

Applicants must possess a bachelor's degree from an accredited four-year program at a college or university.

Qualifications:

Special agent applicants must meet a number of qualifications to be eligible for employment, including standards relating to citizenship, entry age, education, eyesight, hearing, and physical fitness, among others. An extensive physical examination is required during the final screening phase of the application process.

The work of FBI special agents is rigorous and demanding. Special agents must be mentally and physically fit in order to perform surveillance and undercover work, conduct interviews and interrogations, execute search warrants, make arrests, and respond to critical incidents.

Must be a U.S. citizen.

Must be at least 23 years of age, and must have not have reached their 37th birthday at the time of appointment.

Must have a valid U.S. driver's license.

Salary:

Starting pay for an FBI special agent is approximately $61,000.

larly useful if it has been left undisturbed since the incident. However, even when a crime is years old and the scene has not been preserved, he believes it is still worthwhile for him to visit the area. He can see firsthand the local geography and demographics, and this helps him better understand the offender's actions.

To develop a behavioral offender profile, he analyzes all components of the crime, including the victim's characteristics as well as crime scene and forensic evidence. He also tries to determine how the victim might have crossed paths with the offender. To develop the profile, he relies on the experience he has built up from working many cases over the years, plus all the crime scene evidence.

"The work is hard and involves long hours. But it is rewarding to contribute to a successful investigation and see justice served, or to help a family gain some closure,"[44] said Widnman.

"The Cases That Haunt Us"

Former FBI profiler John Douglas says that certain crimes are haunting, perhaps because of the personalities involved, the senselessness of the suffering, the nagging doubts about whether justice was done, or the fact that no one was caught. With each one, questions exist as to whether something was overlooked in the investigation so it could have been solved earlier or had a better outcome.

Etan Patz: Still Missing

Six-year-old Etan Patz left his parents' apartment in the SoHo district of New York City around 8 A.M. on Friday, May 25, 1979. That morning his mother had finally agreed to let him walk the two blocks to the school bus stop alone. They lived in a neighborhood where the residents watched out for the children, so she thought Etan would be safe. She watched him leave and assumed he would board the bus to get to his first-grade class at his school.

When Etan didn't return at 3:30 that afternoon, Julie Patz first started worrying that something was wrong. Then she learned from the friend who usually picked up Etan from the bus stop, and whose daughter was in Etan's class, that he had never boarded the bus that morning, nor had he been at school all day. She called the police and then called her husband, Stanley.

In these cases, time is critical. Statistics show that the chances lessen that he or she will be recovered alive the longer a person is missing. As one police officer said, "the clock is ticking."

"We want our best people moving as fast as they can and using every skill they've got to find missing kids and bring them home safely,"[45] said supervisory special agent Janice Mertz, who heads the Crimes Against Children Unit at FBI headquarters.

New York Police Department detective William Butler received the call about Etan's disappearance at 5:15 P.M. and headed right over to the Patzes' apartment with his partner. By that time, almost ten hours had passed since Etan was last seen. He asked Mr. and Mrs. Patz whether there was any possibility that Etan might have simply decided to skip school and go play somewhere or whether there could have been a simple mix-up as to where Etan thought he should go that day. As an experienced investigator, he knew that could often happen with young children. When these things were ruled out, he organized a search of the area with about 100 officers that evening.

Six-year-old Etan Patz was kidnapped on his way to his school bus stop in New York's SoHo neighborhood on May 25, 1979.

Detailed Search

"We're doing a floor by floor, wall by wall, rooftop by rooftop, backyard by backyard search,"[46] one investigator said at the time. Meanwhile, a police officer stayed with the Patzes at their apartment, in case the kidnapper called them with a ransom demand. Such demands are usually made within the first twenty-four hours after a kidnapping. But no one called, and the searchers didn't find any clues.

It didn't help that this was the Friday night before the Memorial Day holiday weekend. In kidnapping cases, attempts are often made the following day to recreate the victim's travel route during the same time of day that the kidnapping occurred,

to try to find potential witnesses. But the following day was a Saturday on a holiday weekend, so people who might have seen Etan while on their way to work Friday would not be there on a Saturday morning. Another complication of the search was that it had rained during the night, which lessened the ability of the bloodhounds to pick up Etan's scent after smelling a pair of his pajamas.

When no evidence was found, the search area was expanded and a two-part concentrated plan of attack started. First, police boats searched the waterways and police helicopters hovered over a widened search zone, scanning rooftops one by one. Meanwhile officers intensified their house-to-house search, knowing that victims are often kept in the area where they were kidnapped. However, nothing was found.

"Every loft in the area was gone through, not once but three times," one resident said. "Right down to the bottom of our dressers."[47]

Despite public appeal by Etan Patz's parents, including this appearance on the Today *show by his mother Julie in 1981, Etan has never been found.*

Public Appeal

The police then appealed to the public for help in finding Etan, announcing that toll-free tip lines were set up for people to call in with any information they thought might help. Hundreds of posters with Etan's picture were also taped onto windows and telephone polls, with the hope that the posters might jog someone's memory of seeing him. At the time there was no system for television and radio stations to immediately announce a kidnapping, so the flyers were put up to try to alert the public to the crime.

Two witnesses came forward. A woman who lived near the Patz family and a postal carrier both saw Etan as he waited a block away from his house to cross the street. They were both brief sightings, and they took place before the kidnapper snatched Etan. Those two people turned out to be the last known people to ever see the six-year-old.

Parents Are Suspects

Etan's parents had to be ruled out as suspects in his disappearance. Both Mr. and Mrs. Patz were questioned and given polygraph tests, which they passed. Detective Butler thought they seemed to be genuinely distraught by their son's disappearance. It did not seem likely that either had kidnapped Etan as part of a potential custody suit in a divorce or that they could have some other motive. Although parents may complain about having to go through interrogations and take lie detector tests, statistics show that especially when a young child disappears, one of the parents is often responsible.

Investigation Shifts Gears

On June 6 the police department's emergency response to Etan's kidnapping was halted. In kidnapping cases, if the victim or any significant evidence is not found after an initial search, that is a signal to investigators that it is time to pursue other options. It is also seen as a definite setback. While the case would remain open, most of the officers who were pulled in because of the urgency of the case were reassigned to other cases.

Butler has stated that nearly every day he still drives by the Patzes' apartment on his way to work and wonders whether he overlooked anything. This is a common reaction for investigators who work on unsolved kidnappings. However, they hope that someday there will be a break in the case or some new development will occur that will bring the case to a close.

Steps in the Process

Administering a Polygraph (Lie Detector Test)

A polygraph machine is a device that can be used to determine whether a person is lying.

1 Rubber tubes are placed around the person's chest and abdomen, and a blood pressure cuff is placed on the arm. Small metal plates are also attached to the person's fingers.

2 The examiner asks the subject a variety of questions. At first the questions are general, and nonthreatening. The responses provide a baseline measurement of the subject's readings. Then the examiner asks questions about the crime.

3 The examiner watches for changes in the subject's physiological readings. From these results, the examiner can conclude that the subject was truthful, the subject was not truthful, or that the results are inconclusive. Examiners say that when a person lies, his or her body reacts, and it is reflected in peaks that are recorded either by a stylus and moving paper feeder or as a graph on a computer screen. The American Polygraph Association claims that the polygraph's degree of validity is high. However, the examiner must be properly trained, the instrument must be in good working order, and an accepted testing and scoring system must be used.

Suspect Emerges

In 1982, detectives in the Bronx, a borough of New York City, picked up Jose Antonio Ramos after he tried to lure two young boys into the drainage tunnel where he lived. Searching around inside the tunnel, they found pictures of other young boys, mostly blond, like Etan Patz. The detectives were familiar with the unsolved kidnapping, and they decided to ask Ramos about it, knowing they had to phrase their questions carefully. A poorly handled interrogation can make a suspect refuse to talk or lie and tell detectives what he thinks they want to hear.

When detectives asked Ramos about Patz he said he had no knowledge about him. Then he changed his story and said he had dated a woman who had once been hired to walk Patz to school every day. The detectives believed this was how and

 ## Steps in the Process

Taking a Palm Print

1 Cut a 2-inch (5cm) PVC pipe to about twelve (30cm) to fourteen (36cm) inches in length. Secure a piece of plain white paper around the pipe with a rubber band.

2 Ink the subject's hand and roll the hand over the pipe, making sure to get the creases all the way down to the wrist. Then re-ink each hand, and place another sheet of white paper on a flat surface. Roll the hand from the thumb to the little finger, to get the indentations on the meaty part of the side of the hand.

3 Each finger must be printed two more times from different angles. First, print the finger from the base, and then roll to the tip. Then print the finger from one side and roll to the tip and back down to the other side.

4 Ink and press the outer palm, or "karate chop side," of each hand onto another piece of white paper.

when Ramos first saw Patz. Ramos also told them that in 1979 (the year Patz had disappeared) he had a nervous breakdown, and said of the time, "I was ready to explode."[48]

The detectives questioned him more about Patz. At first he was reluctant to talk, but he finally admitted that he saw a boy matching Patz's description about four blocks away from where Patz lived. He even described Patz's distinctive blue tennis shoes with their bright stripes. The detectives believed that the fact that Ramos knew this detail about Patz's shoes was a telltale sign of involvement. Ramos said he brought the boy to his apartment for a short time but later let him go unharmed. At that point, Ramos refused to say any more.

The detectives believed that Ramos had taken Patz and was lying about simply letting him go. They did not have any proof of his guilt, so they had to release him. However, not long afterward, Ramos was sent to prison in Pennsylvania for molesting two young boys.

New Look at Case

In 1985, federal prosecutor Stuart GraBois was assigned to the case. He read all the case files, which mainly focused on Ramos. "What [Ramos] would do is befriend families, befriend a child. One of the things he did was to travel around the United States in a converted bus, giving out matchbox cars and toys ... to young boys, to entice them onto the bus."[49]

GraBois had Ramos brought to New York for questioning. Two detectives from the NYPD Missing Persons Squad, Robert Shaw and Daniel Cavallo, were present at the interview. GraBois was very careful at first to ask Ramos questions about his background and childhood, putting him at ease. Then he asked him what he had done to Patz. Ramos started to sob. "I'll tell you about it. I'll tell you everything. I want to get it off my chest."[50]

Ramos told them he was 90 percent sure that the young boy he took into his apartment the morning Patz had disappeared was indeed Patz. At that point, GraBois and the detectives felt they had the guilty person in front of them. Ramos then stopped, refusing to say more or admitting to sexual assault or murder.

Despite the setback, GraBois became determined to find a way to keep Ramos behind bars and away from any more children. He became deputized in Pennsylvania and tried Ramos on an unrelated child sexual assault case there. The case had gone to trial once before, but was dismissed because of a technicality. Ramos was found guilty and received a ten-year sentence, which was added onto his current sentence.

In 2000, New York police thoroughly searched the building on East 4th Street where Ramos had lived in 1979. They painstakingly went over his apartment as well as the basement, specifically looking for bone fragments they could analyze with DNA tests. They didn't find anything.

"He's a predator," Stanley Patz later said of Ramos in an interview on *60 Minutes II,* "and he should never be allowed to be near children again. He should be kept behind bars until he's too old to walk." Twice a year, on Etan's birthday, October 9, and on May 25, he sends Ramos one of Etan's missing person posters and types on the back, "What have you done with my little boy?"[51]

Today, the Etan Patz case remains unsolved. It is the oldest open missing child case in New York City's history.

A Kidnapping with Witnesses

On October 22, 1989, at 9:15 P.M. eleven-year-old Jacob Wetterling; his ten-year-old brother, Trevor; and his eleven-

Eleven-year-old Jacob Wetterling was kidnapped in Minnesota by a masked gunman while walking home from a convenience store after renting a video.

year-old friend Aaron Larson were returning home from a Tom Thumb convenience store in St. Joseph, Minnesota, after renting a video. They were at a particularly dark stretch of the road when a man wearing a stocking cap stepped out of the darkness. He was carrying a gun.

The man ordered Trevor to turn off his flashlight and for the boys to throw their bikes and scooter into a ditch. After they had done that, he told them to lie flat on the ground on their stomachs. The man then asked them their ages. He also had Aaron and Trevor turn their heads so he could get a good look at their faces. Then he told Aaron and Trevor to run into the nearby woods. He said if they looked back that he would shoot them. The two boys did as they were ordered. When they reached the woods, they finally turned around. By that time the man had grabbed Jacob and disappeared. Later, the two boys described their assailant as a Caucasian man between the ages of 40 and 50 years, about 5 feet 8 inches tall, with a husky build.

Sheriff Charlie Grafft learned about the kidnapping when his pager went off around ten o'clock that night. The crime scene was only about 4 miles (6.5km) from his home, so he got there quickly and saw the bikes and scooter lying in a ditch.

"I looked everything over and said, 'Oh boy, this is going to be a job,'"[52] said Grafft.

He and his deputies searched the rural area with flashlights for about three hours. They found only one faint tire print.

The Search Begins

By midnight, the FBI was called in to the case. The FBI had not always been able to get involved with a kidnapping case so soon, but new laws allowed it to become involved more quickly in cases where foul play was involved. Before long, FBI agents, National Guard troops, and volunteers swarmed over a 36-square-mile (93-square-kilometer) area. At first light, helicopters flew over the area, and bloodhounds sniffed the ground.

"What was unique about it was that we never had a kidnapping where there were witnesses and someone at gunpoint took the child in front of other children,"[53] said Paul McCabe, a Minnesota FBI agent. It was uncharacteristic for a gun to be involved in a child kidnapping. Because sexual predators, or pedophiles, are kidnapping children for sex, they do not want to harm them physically.

By 5:00 A.M., local and national media had been contacted and made aware of Jacob Wetterling's kidnapping. It was hoped that widely publicizing his picture as well as a sketch of the suspect would help someone recognize either of them and notify police.

"Within hours [of the kidnapping]," Wetterling's mother said, "our house was filled with reporters."[54]

The area where Wetterling disappeared was thoroughly searched several times. An extensive flyer campaign was also launched. David Collins, whose son Kevin had been abducted five years earlier and who had founded the Kevin Collins Foundation for Missing Children, flew to the area to offer emotional support. He also helped organize the search effort

An extensive flyer campaign was launched by Wetterling's family soon after his abduction. In spite of there being witnesses to the kidnapping, Jacob has never been found.

so it would be most effective. He was well aware of the importance of a swift resolution to the case. But that did not happen.

Theories and Suspects Emerge

Investigators believe that Jacob was stalked by his captor. His father recalled an incident earlier in the day when he could not find his son at a hockey tryout at an area arena. He said he felt a strange sense of fear for his son. He found the boy a short while later. But after the kidnapping, he wondered whether his son's kidnapper had been in the arena, possibly watching his son.

After two days, police had received numerous tips and had managed to track down 100 potential suspects. One suspect seemed to be particularly promising. Witnesses claimed they had seen a man in his 50s with a large build, white hair, and a receding hairline in two St. Joseph stores, including the Tom Thumb, on the day that Jacob went missing. They remembered him because he had glared at other customers. Another promising lead was that a red Chevette car had been seen in the area that night, leading police to think it might have been the suspect's car. However, in February 2004, the car was identified and the owner was questioned and cleared. It had been an art student who was in St. Joseph looking for things to sketch.

One particularly promising lead in the case occurred when a 19-year-old motorist contacted police. He said he'd seen a man grab a boy and force him into his car in southern Minneapolis. The car then sped away, running a stop sign. In an effort to get more information, police consulted with General Motors designers to try to determine the model and make of the white car the man described. They also had the motorist hypnotized

By the Numbers

85 TO 90

Percentage of missing persons who are juveniles, according to FBI estimates.

The Jacob Wetterling Foundation

Four months after Jacob Wetterling's abduction, his parents founded the Jacob Wetterling Foundation, which is an advocacy group for children's safety. Later, in 1994, Congress passed the Jacob Wetterling Crimes Against Children and Sexually Violent Offender Registration Act, more commonly known as the Jacob Wetterling Act. It was the first law that required states to maintain a registry of convicted sex offenders as well as those who have been found to have committed crimes against children.

to try to get more information. Even after all of their efforts, it proved to be a false lead.

Case Similarities

Two months after Jacob disappeared, a 12-year-old boy was molested about 10 miles (16km) from the place where Jacob had been kidnapped. The boy had been ice-skating and was walking home alone when he was pulled into a car and molested. When the man later dumped the boy out of the car, he told him to run or he would be shot. The boy's description of the man matched the description that the boys had given in the Wetterling kidnapping. The threat of being shot was also used in both instances. Again, a sketch was made, but it did not lead to anything.

Many years later, forensic artists took Jacob's fifth-grade picture and digitally mixed it with photos of his parents and his younger brother to develop an age-progressed photo of what he would look like at age 21. Age-progression computer software and trained forensic artists often are used to create

This computer-enhanced image provided by the National Center for Missing and Exploited Children in 2007 shows what Jacob Wetterling would look like at age 21. Age-progression computer software and trained forensic artists often are used to create results in cold cases.

results in cold cases.

Tips still come in today. "A lot of them are [from] people who always had suspicions that a family member might have been a pedophile and they think we should look at that person for the Wetterling case,"[55] said detective Pam Jenson, who has been assigned to the case.

Some hold out hope that even though so many years have elapsed since the kidnapping, the case one day may be solved. "It's been quite a while but there is always the possibility that someone will have a dose of conscience and may talk before their death," says Lieutenant Dave Nohner, who worked the Wetterling case for eleven years. "There was a huge amount of emotion that ran with this case, and whoever did this has to be carrying huge amounts of baggage."[56]

One investigator wonders whether the aggressive push that night, with hundreds of law enforcement authorities searching the area on foot, on horseback, and in helicopters might have forced the kidnapper from the area. Others disagree, saying the first hours after a kidnapping demand an all-out push to find the victim.

Ultimately the case has resulted in more than 50,000 leads. It has been studied by staff and trainees at the FBI National Academy. During the course of the investigation, at least five different sketches of possible suspects were posted. Still, as of 2007 the case remained unsolved, and the whereabouts of Jacob Wetterling, if still alive, were unknown.

Notes

Chapter One: Is It Kidnapping?

1. Personal interview, police officer Darren Barnett on June 13, 2007, Clute, Texas.

2. Quoted in National Center for Missing & Exploited Children, http://www.missingkids.com.

3. Quoted in Paula Fass, *Kidnapped: Child Abduction in America*. New York: Oxford University Press, 2006, p. 149.

4. Quoted in Fass, p. 149.

5. Quoted in Katherine Pfrommer, "Elsie Abbott," *Oakland (CA) Tribune*, May 6, 2004.

6. Quoted in Crime Library, "Runaways?" http://www.crimelibrary.com/serial_killers/predators/Corll/runaways_5.html.

7. Quoted in Fass, *Kidnapped*, p. 235.

8. Quoted in KTVU.com. "The Kevin Collins Case Turns 20." http://www.ktvu.com/news/2836980/detail.html.

9. Quoted in KTVU.com "The Kevin Collins Case Turns 20."

Chapter Two: Finding the Victim

10. Quoted in Maggie Haberman and Jeane MacIntosh, *Held Captive: The Kidnapping and Rescue of Elizabeth Smart*. New York: Avon, 2003, p. 102.

11. Quoted in "Sister Recounts How She Helped Find Elizabeth Smart," abcnews.go.com, July 21, 2005. http://abcnews.go.com/Primetime/story?id=965906&page=1.

12. Quoted in Ed Smart, Lois Smart, with Laura Morton, *Bringing Elizabeth Home*. New York: Doubleday, 2003, p. 50.

13. Quoted in "Salt Lake City Police: Father of Missing 14-Year Old Given Polygraph," June 10, 2002. www.court-tv.com/archive/news/2002/0610/missingtest_ap.html.

14. Quoted in Tom Smart and Lee Benson, *In Plain Sight*. Chicago: Chicago Review Press, 2005, p. 14.

15. Quoted in Haberman and MacIntosh, *Held Captive*, p. 128.

16. Quoted in Haberman and MacIntosh, *Held Captive*, p. 186.

17. Quoted in Smart, Smart, and Morton, *Bringing Elizabeth Home,* p. 125.

18. Quoted in Haberman and MacIntosh, *Held Captive,* p. 231.

19. Quoted in Smart and Benson, *In Plain Sight,* p. 352, 354.

20. Quoted in Smart, Smart, and Morton, *Bringing Elizabeth Home,* p. 98.

21. Quoted in Crime Library, "Sad Tableau." http://www.crimelibrary.com/notorious_murders/famous/amber_hagerman/2.html.

22. Quoted in Crime Library, "8 Minutes in Texas." http://www.crimelibrary.com/notorious_murders/famous/amber_hagerman/1_index.html.

23. Quoted in Crime Library, "Dead-End Probe." http://www.crimelibrary.com/notorious_murders/famous/amber_hagerman/4.html.

24. Quoted in CBS11tv.com, "Lead Amber Hagerman Investigator Retiring." http://cbs11tv.com/topstories/local_story_059191246.html.

25. Quoted in AMBER Alert Home Page, http://www.amberalert.gov.

26. Quoted in Crime Library, "Pressure on Police." http://www.crimelibrary.com/notorious_murders/famous/amber_hagerman/8.html.

27. Quoted in Crime Library, "Cleveland Case." http://www.crimelibrary.com/notorious_murders/famous/amber_hagerman/9.html.

Chapter Three: Hunting for a Kidnapper

28. Quoted in Connie Fletcher, *Pure Cop.* New York: Villard Books, 1991, p. 7.

29. Quoted in Connie Fletcher, *Every Contact Leaves a Trace.* New York: St. Martin's Press, 2006. p. 14.

30. Quoted in Fletcher, *Pure Cop,* p. 150.

31. Quoted in Jarrett Hallcox and Amy Welch, *Bodies We've Buried: Inside the National Forensic Academy, the World's Top CSI Training School.* New York: Berkley Books, 2006, p. 14.

32. Quoted in Hallcox and Welch, *Bodies We've Buried,* p. xii.

33. Quoted in Fletcher, *Every Contact Leaves a Trace,* p. 16.

34. Quoted in Jane Morrow, managing editor, *Crime Scene Investigation.* New York: Reader's Digest Association, 2004, p. 22.

35. Quoted in Hallcox and Welch, *Bodies We've Buried,* p. 21.

36. Quoted in Fletcher, *Pure Cop,* p. 128.

37. Quoted in Fletcher, *Every Contact Leaves a Trace,* p. 40.

38. Quoted in Court TV News, "A 'Little Girl Lost' Is Found Dead, Allegedly Killed By Neighbor." http://www.courttv.com/trials/westerfield/background_ctv.html.

39. Quoted in Hallcox and Welch, *Bodies We've Buried,* p. 17.

Chapter Four: Profiling Kidnappers

40. Quoted in Katherine Ramsland, *The Forensic Science of C.S.I.* New York: Berkley Boulevard Books, 2001, p. 168.

41. Quoted in Katherine Ramsland, *The Criminal Mind*. Cincinnati, Ohio: Writer's Digest Books, 2002, p. 15.

42. Quoted in Crime Library, "The Mind Hunters," http:/www.crimelibrary.com/criminal_mind/profiling/history_method/6.html.

43. Quoted in John Douglas and Mark Olshaker, *The Cases That Haunt Us*. New York: Pocket Books, 2002, p. 13-14.

44. Quoted in Morrow, *Crime Scene Investigation*, p. 136.

Chapter Five: "The Cases That Haunt Us"

45. Quoted in Federal Bureau of Investigation, "When Kids Go Missing: Our New Teams Will Help Find Them." http://www.fbi.gov/page2/june06/card_teams061606.htm.

46. Quoted in Crime Library, "The Ghost of Etan." http://www.crimelibrary.com/criminal_mind/psychology/child_abduction/11.html.

47. Quoted in Crime Library, "The Ghost of Etan."

48. Quoted in Crime Library, "I Was Ready to Explode." http://www.crimelibrary.com/serial_killers/predators/etan_patz/3.html.

49. Quoted in CBS News, *60 Minutes*, "What Happened to Etan Patz?" http://www.cbsnews.com/stories/2000/05/23/60II/printable198730.shtml.

50. Quoted in CBS News, "What Happened to Etan Patz?"

51. Quoted in Crime Library, "'He's a Predator,'" http://www.crimelibrary.com/serial_killers/predators/etan_patz/5.html.

52. Quoted in Steve Irsay, Court TV News, "The Search for Jacob." www.courttv.com/hiddentraces/wetterling/wetterling_page1.html.

53. Quoted in Irsay, "The Search for Jacob," p. 3.

54. Quoted in Fass, *Kidnapped*, p. 247.

55. Quoted in Irsay, "The Search for Jacob," p. 4.

56. Quoted in Irsay, "The Search for Jacob," p. 4.

For More Information

Books

John Douglas and Mark Olshaker, *The Cases That Haunt Us*. New York: Pocket Books, 2002. This book offers an inside look at how former FBI profiler John Douglas uses his skills to analyze high-profile cases.

Connie Fletcher, *Every Contact Leaves a Trace*. New York: St. Martin's Press, 2006. Fletcher interviewed scores of crime scene investigators, fingerprint technicians, medical examiners, and many other people for this book. It gives a good overview of how people work together to solve crimes.

Jarrett Hallcox and Amy Welch. *Bodies We've Buried: Inside the National Forensic Academy, the World's Top CSI Training School*. New York: Berkley Books, 2006. This book offers a close-up look at how crime scene investigators are trained. Real cases are discussed in the book, to show how various investigative techniques coupled with technology are used to solve crimes.

Katherine Ramsland, *The Forensic Science of C.S.I.* New York: Berkley Boulevard Books, 2001. This book tells how forensic scientists use prints, blood spatter patterns, fibers, hair strands, and other evidence to solve cases.

Periodicals

Vicki Bane and Bill Hewitt, "Saved By Amber Alert," *People Weekly*, July 30, 2007, p. 56.

Web Sites

www.crimelibrary.com—Fascinating detailed accounts of criminals, law enforcement authorities, victims, and crime-solving techniques can be found here. Includes historical as well as current cases.

www.crime-scene-investigator.net—This site has information about evidence collection, crime scene and evidence photography, DNA, fingerprints, among other things, as well as information about careers in crime scene investigation.

Index

Picture Credits

Cover: © Reuters/Corbis

© Ashley Cooper/Corbis, 49

AFP/Getty Images, 25

AP Images, 10, 12, 36, 39, 41, 42, 44, 46, 51, 53, 55, 56, 58, 63, 65, 71, 81, 82, 92

© Bettmann/Corbis, 21

DreamPictures/Getty Images, 14

Getty Images, 30, 31, 33, 35, 60, 62, 68, 70, 73, 75

© 2007/Jupiterimages, 28

Stockbyte/Getty Images, 7

Time & Life Pictures/Getty Images, 8, 17, 87, 89

VCL/Spencer Rowell/Getty Images, 18

About the Author

Jan Burns writes books, articles, and short stories for both children and adults. She received a bachelor's degree in sociology from the University of California at Berkeley. She lives close to Houston, Texas, with her husband, Don, and sons, David and Matt.